W9-BGE-087

MASTERING BASIC SKILLS
FIRST GRADE

Brighter Child®
An imprint of Carson-Dellosa Publishing LLC
Greensboro, North Carolina

An imprint of Carson-Dellosa Publishing LLC
PO Box 35665
Greensboro, NC 27425-5665

© 2006, Carson-Dellosa Publishing LLC. Except as permitted under the United States Copyright Act, no part of this publication may be reproduced, stored, or distributed in any form or by any means (mechanically, electronically, recording, etc.) without the prior written consent of Carson-Dellosa Publishing, LLC. Brighter Child® is an imprint of Carson-Dellosa Publishing LLC.

carsondellosa.com

Printed in the USA. All rights reserved.
ISBN 978-1-4838-0106-3

08-281181151

Table of Contents

Table of Contents

Contents by Skill

Contents by Skill

Introduction

Welcome to *Mastering Basic Skills*. First grade is the year when many children seem to have boundless energy and an incredible desire to learn. Six- and seven-year-olds are thrilled with their emerging ability to read and their heightened mathematical sense. Suddenly, they feel a sense of independence as they practice and perform all their new skills. This book helps reinforce the essential skills learned in first grade through short, fun, and educationally sound activities.

Although six- and seven-year-olds are eager to learn, they also believe that the world revolves around them. It is one of the most egocentric times in a child's life. It is difficult for children at this age to be patient or to delay a response. They simply want every thing and anything immediately. They want to be the best and the first at everything and anything they attempt.

Unfortunately, the world does not always let us be the best or the first, and many six- and seven-year-olds experience high degrees of frustration. Some children will cry easily, while others will demonstrate various tension-releasing behaviors such as pouting, feet-stamping, willfulness, and inflexibility. When a parent recognizes why this behavior is happening and that this behavior is normal, the parent is much more likely to deal with it effectively. Distract and redirect your child into a positive experience. Guide him into a successful moment. Be patient and help teach your child how to be patient. Show him how to express frustration in positive ways and not through negative behaviors.

Although this year is filled with some challenges, it is also a time when children develop a positive self-concept. They learn how to show respect to others and how to respect themselves. Six- and seven-year-olds are becoming more verbally self-expressive and are better able to interpret the feelings of others. They make mistakes, but they are also able to understand and learn from their mistakes.

This is a year when children also become attached to their teachers and seek constant approval from their parents. They need and crave adult guidance, affection, and praise. Enjoy your first grader! Be proud of his accomplishments! Provide constant encouragement!

Everyday Ways to Enrich Learning Experiences

Language Arts

The single most important skill that a child needs for success in school, and later in life, is to be "literate." In other words, children must learn how to read. You can do many things to encourage literacy.

- Read to your child every day and ask your child questions about key details in the text, such as identifying the major characters, settings, and events in the story.
- Give your child a variety of reading materials such as fiction and nonfiction stories, poetry, and informational texts.
- Have your child explain how to use features in books such as table of contents, glossaries, or icons.
- Ask your child to guess what is going to happen next.
- Encourage your child to retell favorite stories or favorite parts of a story.
- Have your child make up a new ending for a story.
- Go to the library and let your child choose new books. Ask your child to explain differences between books that tell stories and books that give information.
- Listen to your child read out loud.
- Write stories together. Have your child illustrate the stories.
- Encourage your child to write about a recent vacation or outing. Have your child recall the sequence of events and use details.
- Write sentences for your child and have him or her add punctuation.
- Play listening games. Ask your child to identify words that share the same sound: initial sounds, ending sounds, vowel sounds, and so on.
- Have your child identify words in the environment, such as on street signs and billboards, in the names of stores, and so on.
- Fill your child's environment with literacy materials like magnetic letters, books, magazines, newspapers, catalogs, paper, pencils, crayons, paint, and CDs of children's music or recorded children's stories.
- Encourage children to draw or write thank-you notes or letters.
- Together, make a scrapbook of first grade memories.

Math & Science

So many toys and puzzles provide young children with early math and science learning experiences. Remember to point out all the ways we use numbers and science in our daily lives. Here are some suggested activities:

- Give your child a magnifying glass to explore his or her environment.
- Provide lots of blocks and other building materials in a variety of geometric shapes. Have your child build things in two different ways.
- Cut out a variety of shapes from construction paper (rectangles, squares, trapezoids, triangles, circles) and practice folding them into halves, fourths, and quarters.
- Have your child practice using numbers "in his head" (mental math). For example: "If you had three cats and one more cat came to visit, how many cats did you have in all? What if two of those cats ran away?"
- Give your child addition problems to solve, then ask him or her to write a subtraction problem to check the answer.
- Use magnetic numbers to create equations with unknown numbers, for example $8 + ? = 11$.
- Play a game of hide and seek with your child where your child must count out loud to 120 while you hide.
- Give your child a handful of paperclips or pennies and encourage him or her to use the objects to measure things around the house.
- Talk about how we use numbers in the real world: telling time, buying groceries, paying bills, and so on.
- Have your child draw on a clock what time he or she wakes up, eats lunch, goes to bed, and so on.
- Take trips to science and children's museums. Ask your child to tell you what he or she learned.
- Take walks and make observations about nature and patterns in nature.
- Encourage your child to track observations in nature and make a bar graph representing the data.

Recommended Books for First Graders

A

The Adventures of Laura and Jack
    by Laura Ingalls Wilder
The Ant and the Elephant by Bill Peet
Are You My Mother? by P.D. Eastman
Arthur's Camp-Out by Lillian Hoban
Arthur's Family Vacation by Marc Brown
Arthur's First Sleepover by Marc Brown
Arthur's Neighborhood by Marc Brown
Arthur's Teacher Trouble by Marc Brown
Aunt Eater's Mystery Vacation
    by Doug Cushman

B

Baseball Brothers by Jean, Dan, and
    Dave Marzollo
A Bear for Miguel by Elaine Marie Alphin
Bear's Hiccups by Marion Dane Bauer
Best Friends by Marcia Leonard
Best Friends for Frances by Russell Hoban
The Best Way to Play by Bill Cosby
Big Bad Bruce by Bill Peet
The Boy with the Helium Head
    by Phyllis Reynolds Naylor
Bright Lights, Little Gerbil by Stephanie Spinner
    and Ellen Weiss
Buffalo Bill and the Pony Express
    by Eleanor Coerr
Buford, the Little Bighorn by Bill Peet

C

The Caboose Who Got Loose by Bill Peet
*Cam Jansen and the Triceratops Pops
    Mystery* by David A. Adler
Cinderella, illustrated by Marcia Brown
Come Down Now, Flying Cow!
    by Timothy Roland
Commander Toad and the Voyage Home
    by Jane Yolen

D

Danny and the Dinosaur Go to Camp
    by Syd Hoff
Do You Want to Be My Friend? by Eric Carle
The Dog That Called the Pitch
    by Matt Christopher
Don't Forget the Bacon! by Pat Hutchins

F

Father Bear Comes Home
    by Else Holmelund Minarik,
    illustrated by Maurice Sendak
Five Little Monkeys Jumping on the Bed,
    retold and illustrated by Eileen Christelow
Flossie and the Fox by Patricia C. McKissack
Frog and Toad All Year by Arnold Lobel
Frog and Toad Are Friends by Arnold Lobel
Funnybones by Janet and Allan Ahlberg

G

The Gingerbread Boy by Paul Galdone
The Golly Sisters Ride Again by Betsy Byars
Good Night, Good Knight
    by Shelley Moore Thomas
Good-night, Owl! by Pat Hutchins
Gorky Rises by William Steig

H

Harold and the Purple Crayon
    by Crockett Johnson
*Henry and Mudge and Annie's Perfect Pet:
    The Twentieth Book of Their Adventures*
    by Cynthia Rylant
*Henry and Mudge and the Sneaky Crackers:
    The Sixteenth Book of Their Adventures*
    by Cynthia Rylant
*Higglety Pigglety Pop! Or, There Must Be More
    to Life* by Maurice Sendak
Hour of the Olympics by Mary Pope Osborne

I

I Know an Old Lady Who Swallowed a Fly,
    retold and illustrated by Nadine Bernard
    Westcott
If You Give a Moose a Muffin
    by Laura Joffe Numeroff
If You Give a Mouse a Cookie
    by Laura Joffe Numeroff
Inside, Outside, Upside Down by Stan
    and Jan Berenstain
Ira Sleeps Over by Bernard Waber

J

Jethro and Joel Were a Troll by Bill Peet
Joshua James Likes Trucks by Catherine Petrie

L

Last One in Is a Rotten Egg by Leonard Kessler
Lightning Liz by Larry Dane Brimner
Lilly's Purple Plastic Purse by Kevin Henkes
Little Wolf, Big Wolf by Matt Novak

M

Make Way for Ducklings by Robert McCloskey
Mama's Birthday Surprise by Elizabeth Spurr
Marmee's Surprise: A Little Women Story,
    adapted by Monica Kulling, based on the
    novel by Louisa May Alcott
Meow!, retold and illustrated by Katya Arnold
Messy Bessey by Patricia and
    Frederick McKissack
Mike Mulligan and His Steam Shovel
    by Virginia Lee Burton
Miss Nelson Is Missing! by Harry Allard and
    James Marshall
The Mitten: A Ukrainian Folktale, adapted
    and illustrated by Jan Brett
The Mixed-up Chameleon by Eric Carle
Monkey Trouble by David Martin
Mouse Mess by Linnea Riley
My Brother, Ant by Betsy Byars
My Name Is María Isabel by Alma Flor Ada

N

*Nate the Great and Me: The Case of the
    Fleeing Fang* by Marjorie Weinman
    Sharmat
No Jumping on the Bed! by Tedd Arnold

O

Ox-Cart Man by Donald Hall

P

Petunia by Roger Duvoisin
Picnic with Piggins by Jane Yolen
Pinky and Rex and the New Baby
    by James Howe
Pioneer Cat by William H. Hooks
Play Ball, Amelia Bedelia by Peggy Parish
The Polar Express by Chris Van Allsburg

R

The Rainbow Fish by Marcus Pfister
Rats on the Roof and Other Stories
    by James Marshall

The Relatives Came by Cynthia Rylant
Roland, the Minstrel Pig by William Steig
Rooster's Off to See the World by Eric Carle
Rosie's Walk by Pat Hutchins

S

*Silver Packages: An Appalachian Christmas
    Story* by Cynthia Rylant
Skip to My Lou, adapted and illustrated by
    Nadine Bernard Westcott
Sleep-Over Mouse by Mary Packard
Smasher by Dick King-Smith
Something Queer in the Cafeteria
    by Elizabeth Levy
Song and Dance Man by Karen Ackerman
Song Lee and the Hamster Hunt by Suzy Kline
Stone Soup: An Old Tale, retold and illustrated
    by Marcia Brown
The Stories Huey Tells by Ann Cameron
The Story of Ferdinand by Munro Leaf
Strega Nona: An Old Tale, retold and
    illustrated by Tomie de Paola
Strega Nona's Magic Lessons
    by Tomie de Paola

T

The Tales of Peter Rabbit and Benjamin Bunny,
    adapted by Sindy McKay from the stories
    of Beatrix Potter
Three by the Sea by Edward Marshall
Time for Bed? by Susan Hood
The Three Little Pigs, illustrated by Eileen Grace
The Town Mouse and the Country Mouse,
    retold and illustrated by Helen Craig

V

Veronica by Roger Duvoisin
The Very Busy Spider by Eric Carle
The Very Clumsy Click Beetle by Eric Carle
The Very Hungry Caterpillar by Eric Carle
The Very Quiet Cricket by Eric Carle

W

Wizard and Wart in Trouble
    by Janice Lee Smith
Wolfmen Don't Hula Dance by Debbie Dadey
    and Marcia Thornton Jones

First Grade Skills Checklist

This list is an overview of some of the key skills learned in first grade. When using this list, please keep in mind that the curriculum will vary across the United States, as will how much an individual teacher is able to teach over the course of one year. The list will give you an overview of the majority of first grade skills and assist you in motivating, guiding, and helping your child maintain or even increase skills.

Language Arts/Reading

Recognizes uppercase letters..❑
Recognizes lowercase letters...❑
Can print uppercase letters correctly...❑
Can print lowercase letters correctly..❑
Knows alphabetical sequence...❑
Recognizes beginning consonant sounds ....❑
Recognizes final consonant sounds..❑
Recognizes short vowel sounds ....❑
Recognizes long vowel sounds...❑
Knows L blends: bl, cl, fl, gl, pl, sl ....❑
Knows beginning blends: sk, sm, sn, sp, st, sw, tw ....❑
Knows R blends: br, cr, dr, fr, gr, pr, tr ....❑
Knows digraphs: ch, sh, th, ng ....❑
Recognizes r-controlled vowels: ar, er, ir, or, ur..❑
Can sound out simple words ....❑
Can identify characters in a story...❑
Can identify the main idea of a story ....❑
Can identify the setting of a story...❑
Can identify the conclusion of a story...❑
Uses letter sounds to write words..❑
Draws illustrations to match sentences...❑
Can identify compound words ....❑
Can identify nouns ....❑
Can identify proper nouns ....❑
Can identify pronouns ....❑
Can identify verbs ....❑
Can identify linking verbs: am, is, are, was, were ....❑
Uses punctuation correctly: period, question mark, exclamation point.................❑
Recognizes rhyming words...❑
Recognizes antonyms, synonyms, and homonyms ....❑
Is beginning to read and write for pleasure ....❑

Math

Counts and recognizes numbers to 120..□

Counts by 2s to 100..□

Counts by 5s to 100..□

Counts by 10s to 100..□

Completes simple patterns ....□

Sorts by one or two attributes ....□

Can sequence events ....□

Can name eight basic shapes ....□

Knows addition facts to 20..□

Knows subtraction facts to 20...□

Can write number sentences using +, −, and =...................................□

Knows addition facts to 18..□

Knows subtraction facts to 18...□

Can read and create a graph..□

Knows ordinal numbers (first–tenth) ....□

Reads number words ....□

Understands place value in the ones place ....□

Understands place value in the tens place..□

Understands place value in the hundreds place ....□

Adds two-digit numbers, no regrouping ....□

Subtracts two-digit numbers, no regrouping ....□

Adds three-digit numbers, no regrouping..□

Subtracts three-digit numbers, no regrouping.....................................□

Performs column addition with three single-digit numbers ....□

Recognizes money: penny, nickel, dime, quarter, half-dollar ....□

Knows the value of money: penny, nickel, dime, quarter, half-dollar...............□

Can count money using pennies, nickels, and dimes...............................□

Can perform money addition problems using a decimal point.......................□

Can tell time on the hour ....□

Can tell time on the half hour ....□

Can measure using inches...□

Can measure using centimeters ....□

Can identify fractions: 1/2, 1/3, 1/4...□

Uses problem-solving strategies to complete math problems ....□

First Grade Word Lists

after	can	get	I	new	quit	talk	want
all	can't	girl	in	nice		teacher	was
am	car	give	is	night	rain	tell	we
and	children	go	it	no	ride	that	went
animal	come	good		not		the	what
are			jump		said	them	when
at	day	had		of	saw	there	where
	did	has	kick	off	school	they	who
be	do	have		old	see	thing	why
because	down	he	like	on	she	this	will
best		her	little	out	sister	to	with
big	eat	here	look	over	some		won't
boy		him				up	
brother	favorite	his	made	people		us	you
but	for	house	make	play			your
	friend	how	me	pretty		very	
	from		my				zoo
	fun						

Long Vowels

Initial a	Initial e	Initial i	Initial o	Initial u	Medial a	Medial e
able	ecology	I	obey	uniform	baby	being
acre	equal	icy	oboe	unify	basis	cedar
agent	ether	idea	ocean	unique	crazy	depot
apex	even	iodine	odor	unit	flavor	female
April	evil	iris	okra	united	hazy	legal
apron		item	omit	universe	label	meter
Asia		ivory	open	university	labor	prefix
			over	usual	ladle	recent
				utilize	lady	secret
					navy	zebra
					paper	
					station	
					vapor	

Medial i	Medial o	Medial u	Final e	Final o	Final u
bicycle	broken	bugle	be	ago	emu
climate	moment	cubic	he	also	guru
dinosaur	October	cupid	maybe	cargo	menu
giant	poem	fuel	me	echo	tutu
lion	program	future	she	hello	
pilot	total	human	we	hero	
rifle		humid		piano	
silent		humor		volcano	
spider		museum		zero	
tiny		puny			
title		pupil			
triangle					

Short Vowels

Initial a	Initial e	Initial i	Initial o	Initial u
act	edge	if	October	ugly
add	egg	igloo	octopus	umbrella
after	elbow	ill	odd	uncle
alligator	elephant	in	off	uncover
alphabet	elevator	inch	offer	under
animal	elf	Indian	office	underwear
answer	elk	ink	olive	undress
ant	elm	insect	omelet	unhappy
antelope	envelope	instrument	operation	until
apple	Eskimo	interest	ostrich	up
ask	ever	introduce	otter	us
astronaut	every	invent	ox	
at	everyone	invite	oxygen	
ax	except	it		
	explain	itch		

Medial a		Medial e		Medial i		Medial o		Medial u	
bag	grab	bed	men	bring	milk	block	job	buck	just
band	grass	beg	nest	chin	mitt	bog	jog	bud	luck
basket	had	bell	peg	dig	mix	box	lock	bug	mud
bat	ham	belt	pen	dish	pick	chop	log	bump	mug
batch	hand	bench	red	ditch	pig	clock	lost	bunch	must
cab	hat	bent	rest	fig	pin	clot	lot	bus	nuts
can	hatch	best	set	fish	pinch	cloth	mop	cub	plum
cat	patch	bet	sled	fist	ring	cob	moth	cuff	rub
class	path	desk	spell	fit	rip	cost	not	cup	rug
crab	quack	guess	spent	grin	ship	cot	ox	cut	run
dad	ranch	help	tent	hid	sick	dock	pop	drum	rust
fan	scratch	hen	vest	hitch	silly	dog	rob	duck	shrunk
fat	spank	jelly	west	kit	sing	doll	rock	dump	skunk
flag	stack	jet	wet	jig	sink	drop	rocker	dust	stump
gas	tracks	leg	when	lid	sip	flop	shop	hug	sunk
glass		let	yet	lift	six	fog	sock	hunt	truck
				limb	skinny	fox	spot	jug	trunk
				limp	sticks	frog	stop	jump	tub
				lips		golf	top		
						hog	tot		
						hot			

Patterns

Continue each pattern.

Great job Avani!!   Muy bien Amiga.

Symbols

1.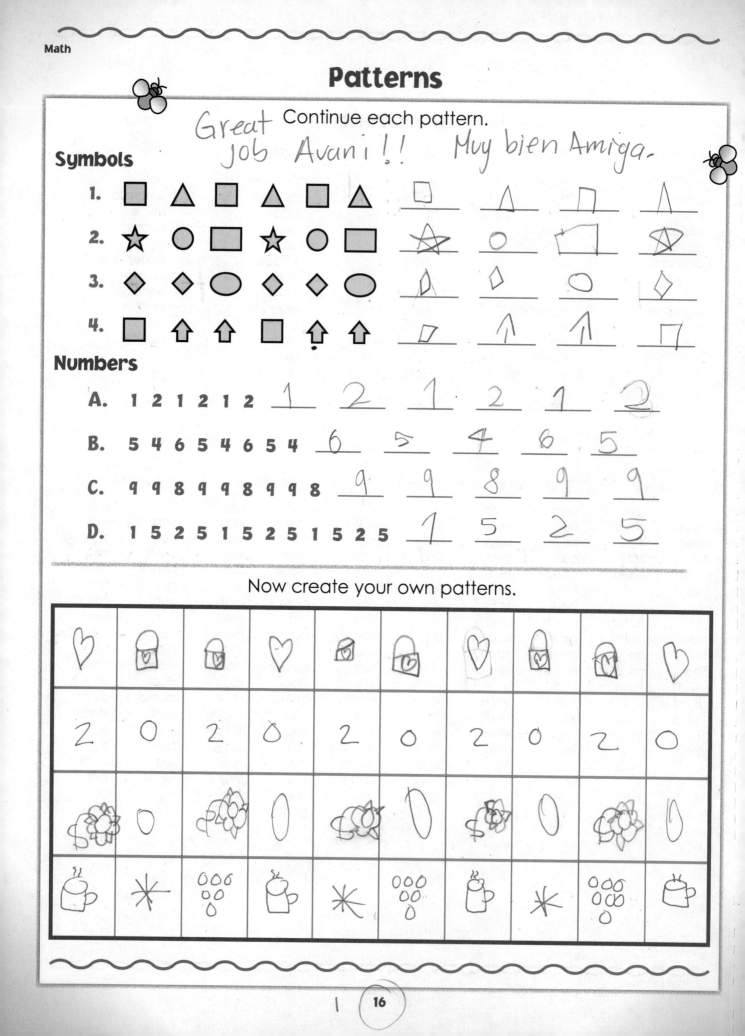

2.

3.

4.

Numbers

A. 1 2 1 2 1 2   1 2 1 2 1 2

B. 5 4 6 5 4 6 5 4   6 5 4 6 5

C. 9 9 8 9 9 8 9 9 8   9 9 8 9 9

D. 1 5 2 5 1 5 2 5 1 5 2 5   1 5 2 5

Now create your own patterns.

Uppercase Letters

Trace and print the uppercase letters.

very nice !!

A A A A B B B B C C C C

D D D D E E E E F F F F

G G G G H H H H I I I I

J J J J K K K K L L L L

M M M M N N N N O O O O

P P P P Q Q Q R R R R

S S S S T T T T U U U U

V V V V W W W W

X X X X Y Y Y Y Z Z Z Z

Lowercase Letters

Trace and print the lowercase letters.

vowels → vocales = a, e, i, o, u, y

a a a a   b b b b   c c c c

d d d d   e e e e   f f f f

g g g   h h h h   i i i i

j j j j   k k k k   l l l l

m m m m   n n n n   o o o o

p p p p   q q q q   r r r r

s s s s   t t t t   u u u u

v v v v   w w w w

x x x x   y y y y   z z z z

Hundred Chart

1	2	3	4	5	6	7	8	9	10
11	12	13	14	15	16	17	18	19	20
21	22	23	24	25	26	27	28	29	30
31	32	33	34	35	36	37	38	39	40
41	42	43	44	45	46	47	48	49	50
51	52	53	54	55	56	57	58	59	60
61	62	63	64	65	66	67	68	69	70
71	72	73	74	75	76	77	78	79	80
81	82	83	84	85	86	87	88	89	90
91	92	93	94	95	96	97	98	99	100
101	102	103	104	105	106	107	108	109	110
111	112	113	114	115	116	117	118	119	120

Beginning Consonant Review (Part 1)

Circle the correct beginning sound.

b d l

c t d

u v w

n z v

s f h

g p d

q r p

e s n

t l h

n o u

m r n

k l h

Counting by 1s

Help Fuzzy find her bone.
Start at 1. Count by 1s and trace your path.

1	2	0	12	13	14	5	40	43	44
12	3	13	11	39	15	7	25	26	27
16	4	5	10	36	16	38	24	41	28
14	20	6	9	18	17	22	23	45	29
31	24	7	8	19	20	21	34	42	30

Wow!
You did a great job!

Beginning Consonant Review (Part 2)

Circle the correct beginning sound.

100%

e (c) d   f p (d)   (f) t h

n u (m)   u x (v)   (q) g p

t (l) h   (y) j g   p (j) t

u l (t)   (b) d t   t (k) h

Counting by 2s and 5s

Count by 2s. Fill in the missing numerals in each row.

A. 2 4 6 8 10 **12**

B. **14** 16 18 **20** 22 24

C. 28 **30** 31 33 **36** 37

D. **40** 42 44 **46** 48 50

Count by 5s. Fill in the missing numerals in each row.

E. **5** 10 15 **20** 30

F. **35** 40 **45** 50 55 60

G. **70** 72 80 **85** 90 95

H. **55** 60 62 70 **75** 80

23 7

Beginning Consonant Review (Part 3)

Write the correct beginning sound.

ball	pig	net	fox
kite	lamp	cat	sun
hat	duck	ring	moon
goat	van	jar	wig

Ending Consonant Review

Circle the correct ending sound.

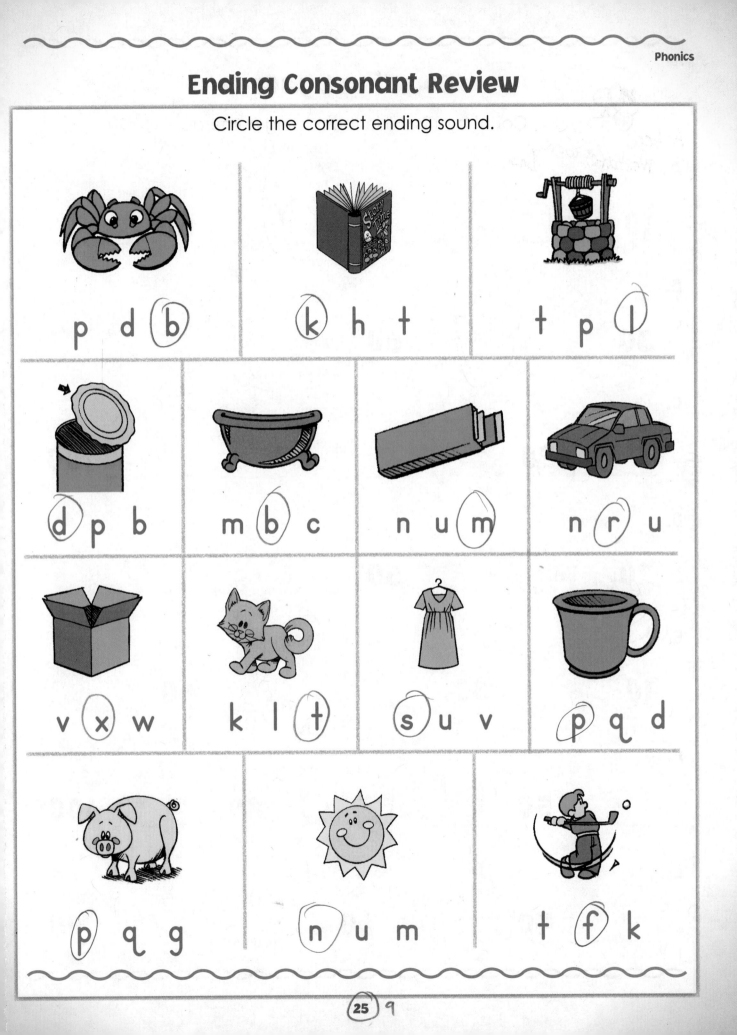

p d (b)

(k) h t

t p (l)

(d) p b

m (b) c

n u (m)

n (r) u

v (x) w

k l (t)

(s) u v

(p) q d

(p) q g

(n) u m

t (f) k

Counting by 10s

Count by 10s. Fill in the missing numerals.

A few mistakes were done

A. 10 _20_ _30_ 40 _50_ 60 _70_

B. 30 _40_ _50_ 60 _70_ _80_ _90_

C. _40_ 50 _60_ _70_ _80_ _90_ 100

D. 20 _30_ _60_ 50 _60_ _70_ _80_

E. 10 _20_ 30 _40_ _50_ 60 _70_

F. _40_ 50 _60_ _70_ 80 _90_ 100

G. _30_ 40 _50_ 60 _70_ _80_ 90

26   10

Beginning and Ending Consonant Review

Write the correct beginning and ending sounds.

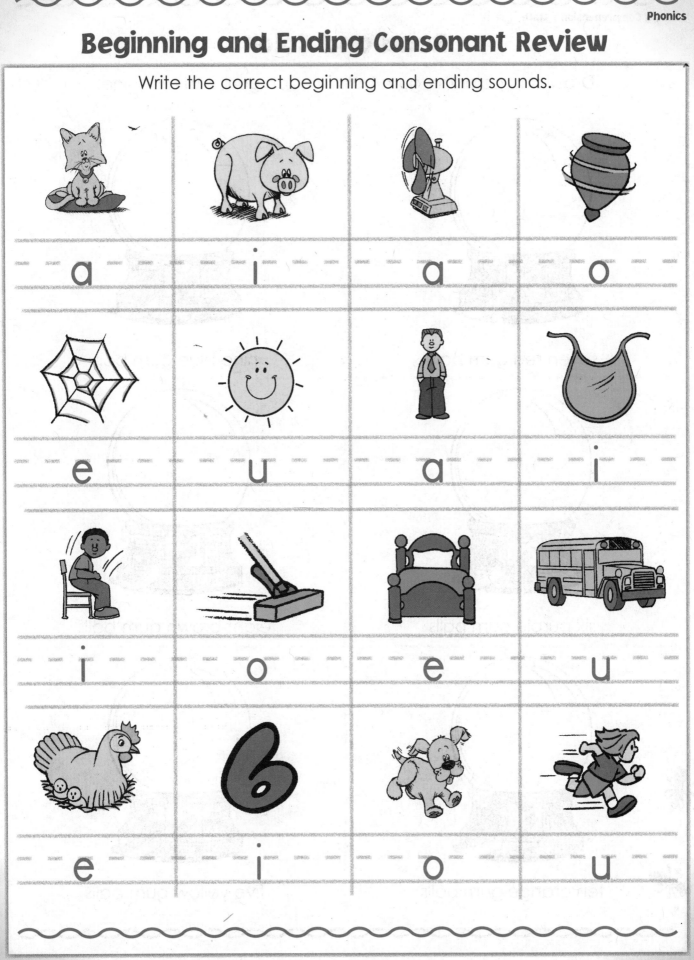

Read and Color

Draw and color the gum balls in each gum ball machine.

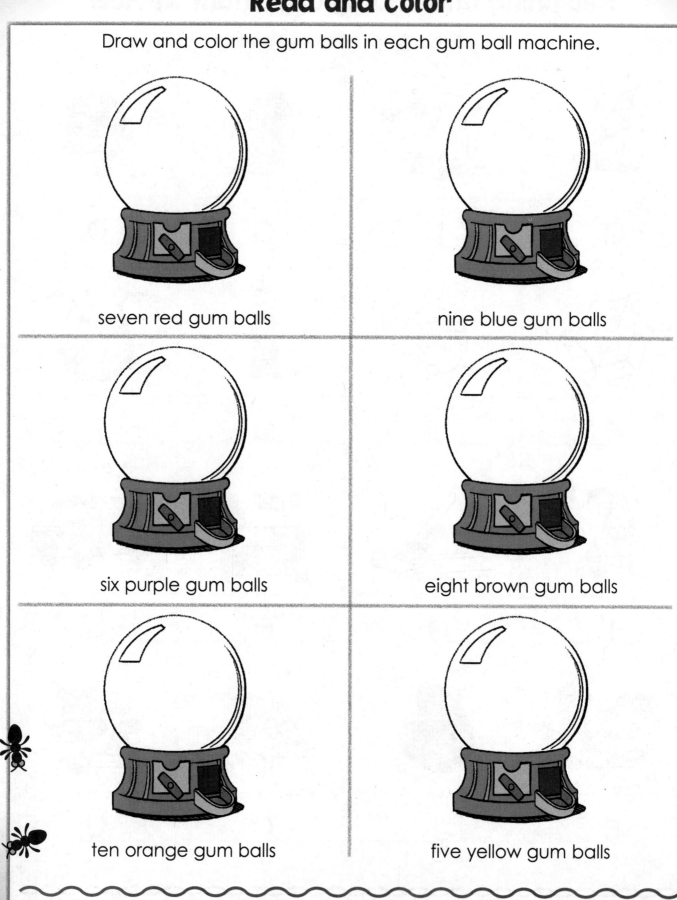

seven red gum balls

nine blue gum balls

six purple gum balls

eight brown gum balls

ten orange gum balls

five yellow gum balls

Cut-and-Paste Respect

Cut out the eight squares at the bottom of the page.
Paste each activity to show whether it demonstrates
respect to self, property, others, or the environment.

Self	Property	Others	Environment

Return library
books on time.

Exercise.

Put things back
where they belong.

Pick up litter.

Share toys.

Recycle.

Eat healthy food.

Take turns.

My Secret Code
Riddle Book

By

Detective

1

Use the secret code to solve the riddle.

which side of a chicken has the most feathers?

The

Secret Code

♣ = T   ☘ = O   ♥ = U

🍓 = D   ☺ = S   🐝 = I

🌲 = T   ♪ = E

3

Use the secret code to solve the riddle.

What kind of animal is always found at a baseball game?

A _____

Secret Code

= A = T = B

Use the secret code to solve the riddle.

What kind of cup is good to eat?

A _____

Secret Code

= U = K = E

= C = A = P

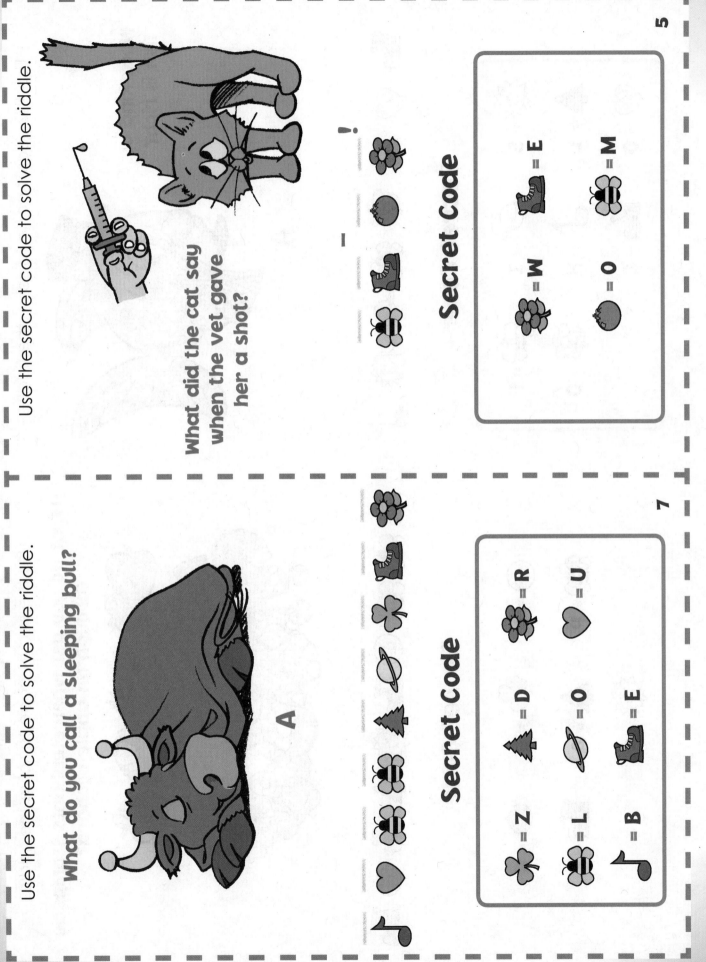

Use the secret code to solve the riddle.

What did the cat say
when the vet gave
her a shot?

_ _ _ _ !

Secret Code

= W   = E

= O   = M

Use the secret code to solve the riddle.

what do you call a sleeping bull?

A _ _ _ _ _ _ _ _

Secret Code

= Z   = D   = R

= L   = O   = U

= B   = E

Use the secret code to solve the riddle.

**What kind of
fish is rich?**

A

Secret Code

🌞 = S   🪐 = I
▲ = L   ♪ = H   🌸 = D   🐝 = F
❤ = O   👟 = G

6

Use the secret code to solve the riddle.

**What do you get when elephants stampede
through an apple orchard?**

Secret Code

🙂 = L   ♣ = U   🥔 = C
🐝 = P   ▲ = A   👟 = E
🌞 = S

8

Nouns (Naming Words)

A **noun** is a word that names a person, place, or thing.

Cut and paste the picture of each noun where it belongs.

Person	Place	Thing

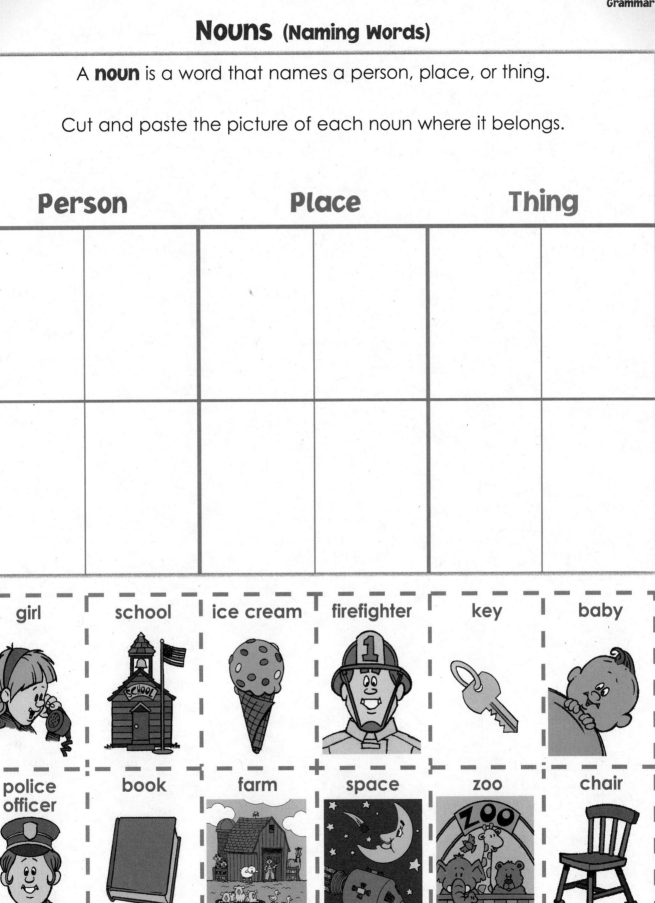

girl   school   ice cream   firefighter   key   baby

police officer   book   farm   space   zoo   chair

Practice Using Nouns

Read each sentence. Write the correct noun from the word list on the line. You will not use all of the words.

Word List

baby	doctor	teacher
nest	school	chair
hospital	dentist	car
woods	pencil	cowboy
piano	apple	store

1. This is a **thing** used to make music.

2. This **person** checks your teeth.

3. This **place** sells things you need.

4. This is a **thing** you use to write.

5. This **person** helps you learn at school.

6. This **place** is where children go to learn.

7. This is a **thing** in which a bird lays eggs.

8. This **person** works in a hospital.

Story Web

Read your favorite story. Describe it by filling in the story web below with words, sentences, or pictures.

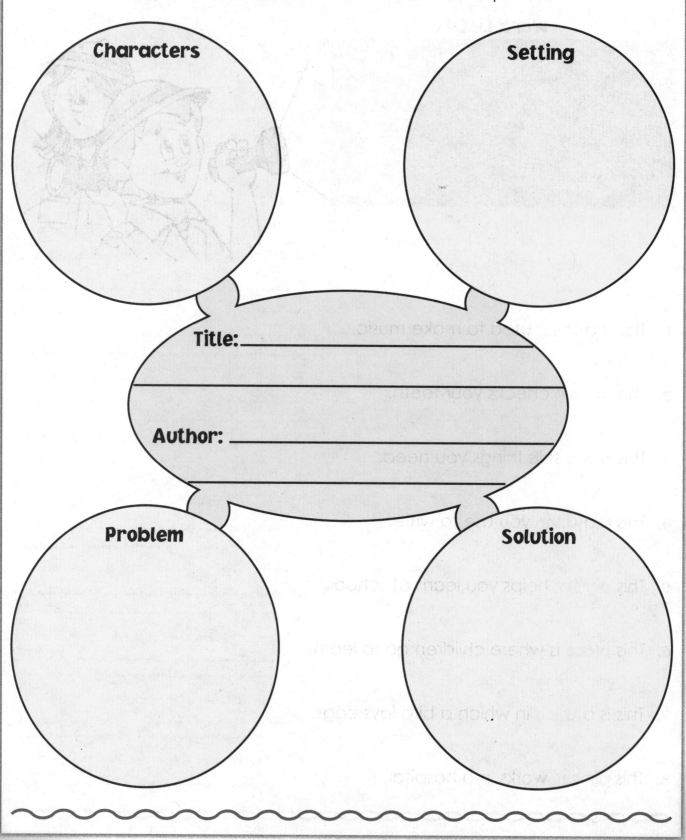

Characters

Setting

Title: _____

_____

Author: _____

Problem

Solution

Short ă

Say the words. Listen to the short sound of the vowel **a**.

căp 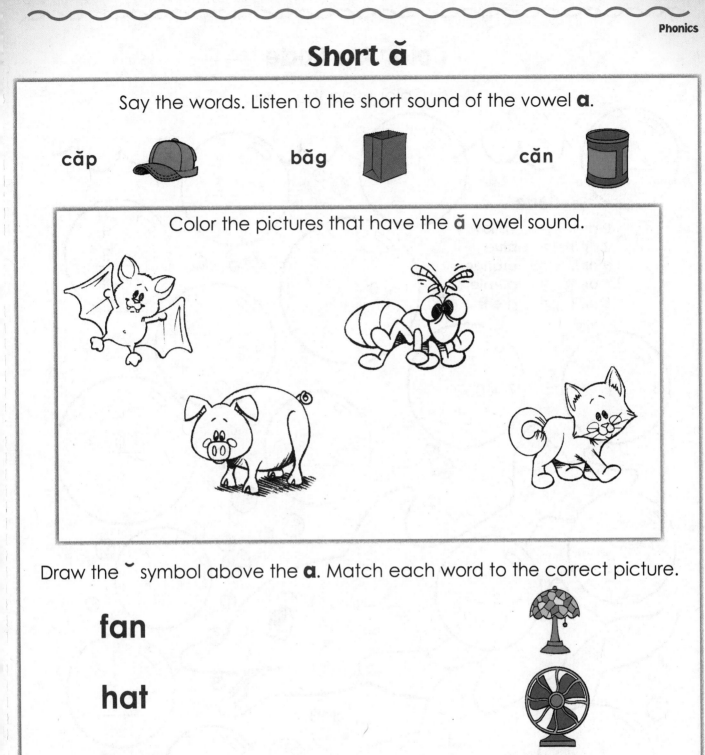 băg căn

Color the pictures that have the **ă** vowel sound.

Draw the ˘ symbol above the **a**. Match each word to the correct picture.

fan

hat

lamp

Write three words that have the short **ă** sound as in **pan**.

Color by Code

Add. Color using the code.

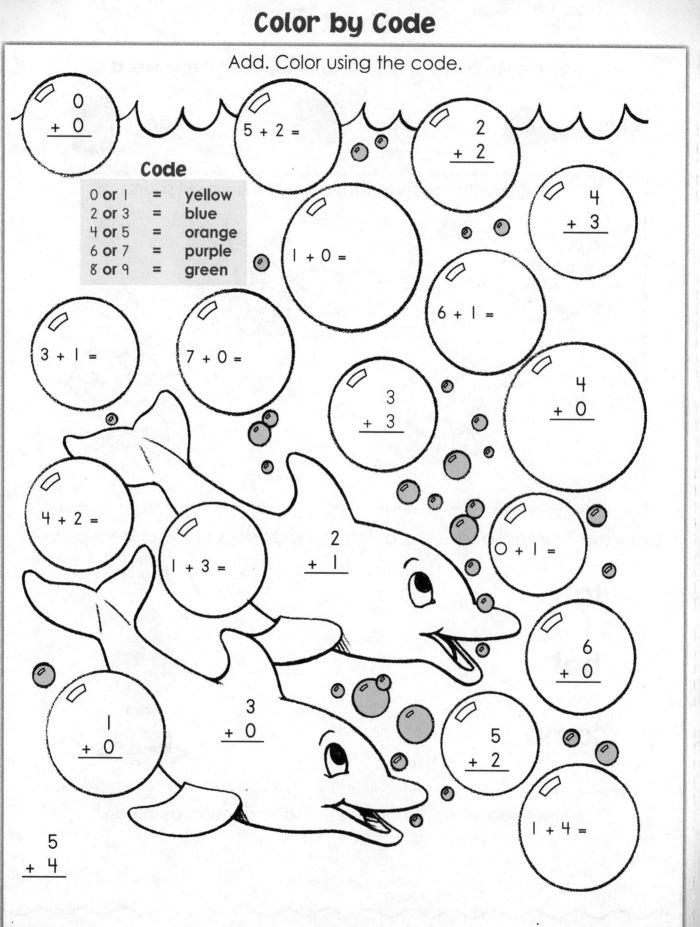

$$0 + 0$$

$$5 + 2 =$$

$$2 + 2$$

$$4 + 3$$

Code

0 or 1	=	yellow
2 or 3	=	blue
4 or 5	=	orange
6 or 7	=	purple
8 or 9	=	green

$$1 + 0 =$$

$$6 + 1 =$$

$$3 + 1 =$$

$$7 + 0 =$$

$$3 + 3$$

$$4 + 0$$

$$4 + 2 =$$

$$1 + 3 =$$

$$2 + 1$$

$$0 + 1 =$$

$$6 + 0$$

$$1 + 0$$

$$3 + 0$$

$$5 + 2$$

$$1 + 4 =$$

$$5 + 4$$

Capitalization

Capitalize the **first word in a sentence, days of the week, months,** and **proper names** of people and places.

Example: **W**e took **R**honda to **N**ew **Y**ork on a **F**riday in **J**une.

Circle the letters that need to be capitalized.

1. she played ball on our team.

2. dr. sharma is our dentist.

3. do you know paul brown?

4. we are going to atlanta in december.

5. may we go to the park on sunday?

6. on tuesday we can go swimming.

7. are you going with us on wednesday?

8. please call robin stuart tonight.

9. we are traveling to california on friday.

10. have you met my friend maria?

11. marsha and matthew are sister and brother.

12. our teacher this year is mr. perry.

Yummy Good! (Addition to 10)

Add.

$4 + 1 =$

$5 + 4 =$

$1 + 6 =$

$2 + 5 =$

$3 + 4 =$

$3 + 6 =$

$5 + 5 =$

$5 + 3 =$

$0 + 4 =$

$4 + 6 =$

BRAIN BUILDER

How many honey pots
have a sum less than 6? _____

Short ĕ

Say the words. Listen to the short sound of the vowel **e**.

wĕt

bĕll

nĕt

Color the pictures that have the ĕ vowel sound.

10

Complete each sentence.

Word List

leg

neck

nest

fell

1. A robin builds its _____ in a tree.

2. I hurt my _____ when I _____ off my bike.

3. A giraffe has a long _____ .

Write three words that have the short ĕ sound as in **pen**.

_____

Short ĭ

Say the words. Listen to the short sound of the vowel **i**.

sĭx   **6**   pĭg   lĭps

Color the pictures that have the **ĭ** vowel sound.

Change the highlighted vowel to the letter **i** to make a new word.
Write the new word. Draw the ˘ symbol above the letter **i**.

bug _____   hall _____

let _____   fog _____

Write three words that have the short **ĭ** sound as in **pig**.

_____

_____

Addition Story Problems

A. Amy went to the museum.
She saw **5** dinosaurs in one room
and **3** dinosaurs in another room.
How many dinosaurs did Amy see in all?

_____ + _____ = ☐

B. Stegasaurus laid **4** eggs.
Allosaurus laid **4** eggs, too.
What was the total number of eggs laid by the dinosaurs?

_____ + _____ = ☐

C. Put 12 counters in a row. Using your pencil, divide the counters into two sets. Start by putting your pencil after the first counter on the left, like this:

On another sheet of paper, write the combination you see (1 + 11).
Now move your pencil one counter to the right.
Write this combination under the first one you wrote.
Continue until you have moved your pencil all the way to the right.
Do you see any patterns?

Color the Farm

Say the name of everything you see in the picture.
Follow the directions.

1. Color the dog brown.
2. Color the pond blue.
3. Color the cow black.
4. Color the barn red.
5. Color the hen orange.
6. Color the tree green.

Flying High! (Subtraction to 10)

Subtract. Color using the code. Then color the rest of the picture.

Code

0 or 1 = blue
2 or 3 = yellow

5 − 3 =

4 − 2 =

6 − 5 =

4 − 1 =

$$\begin{array}{r} 7 \\ -\ 4 \\ \hline \end{array}$$

6 − 4 =

$$\begin{array}{r} 4 \\ -\ 1 \\ \hline \end{array}$$

$$\begin{array}{r} 7 \\ -\ 6 \\ \hline \end{array}$$

$$\begin{array}{r} 3 \\ -\ 1 \\ \hline \end{array}$$

Verbs (Action Words)

A **verb** is a word that shows action.

Examples: walk   I **walk** to school every day.

ride   My friend **rides** the bus.

Write the **verb** from the word list that matches each picture.

Word List

drive
cook
eat
sew
swim
run

Finish each sentence with a **verb** from the word list.

1. Mr. Henry _____ hard on his farm.

2. He _____ all the hungry pigs.

3. He _____ corn and oats.

4. He _____ the cows two times each day.

Word List

milks

works

plants

feeds

Number Sentence Story Problems

Write a number sentence for each story problem.

A. Trevor invited **5** boys to his birthday party.
He also invited **4** girls.
How many children did he invite in all?

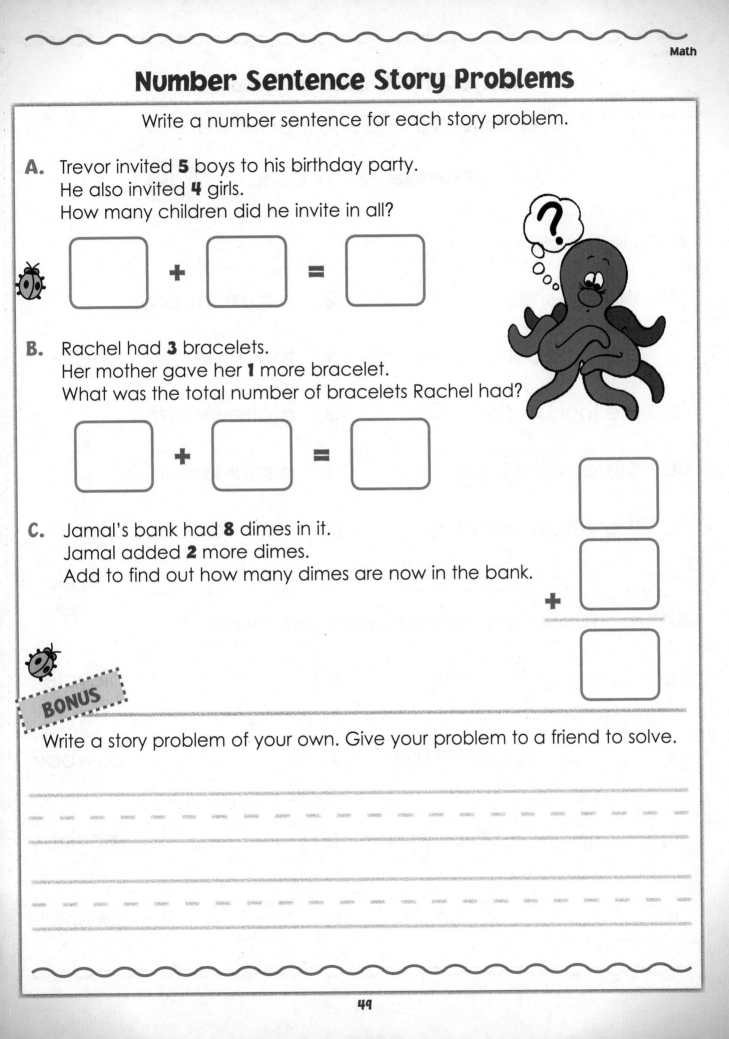

[ ] **+** [ ] **=** [ ]

B. Rachel had **3** bracelets.
Her mother gave her **1** more bracelet.
What was the total number of bracelets Rachel had?

[ ] **+** [ ] **=** [ ]

C. Jamal's bank had **8** dimes in it.
Jamal added **2** more dimes.
Add to find out how many dimes are now in the bank.

[ ]
[ ]
+
[ ]

BONUS

Write a story problem of your own. Give your problem to a friend to solve.

Adjectives (Describing Words)

An **adjective** is a word used to describe a noun.

Example: the red balloon

A. Circle the adjectives.

1. the big shoe

2. a tiny pebble

3. the loud radio

4. the colorful dress

5. the yellow bananas

6. a fuzzy puppy

7. the three elephants

8. a chewy taffy

9. a sour lemon

10. the two cupcakes

B. Write an adjective on the blank beside each noun.

1. _____ dog

2. _____ squirrel

3. _____ carrots

4. _____ daisy

1. _____ bicycle

2. _____ cowboy

3. _____ monkey

4. _____ seashell

Pronouns

A **pronoun** is a word used in place of a noun.

Example: Elena is my cousin.
She is my cousin.

Choose the correct pronoun from the word list to replace the
noun phrase in each ball. Write the pronoun on the blank.

Word List

he
she
it
we
they

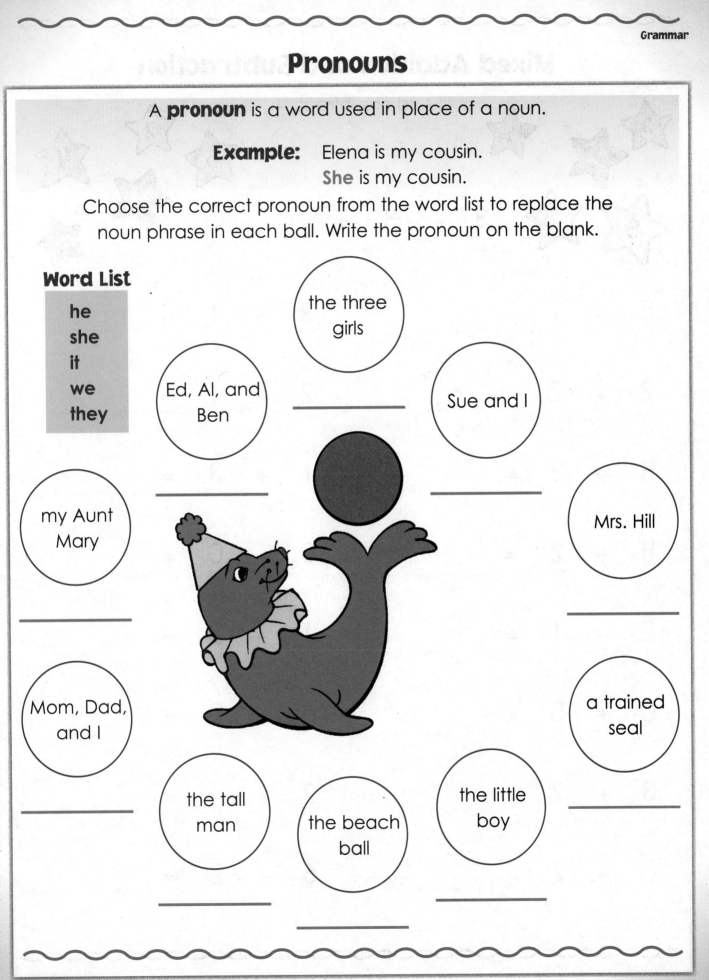

the three
girls

Ed, Al, and
Ben

Sue and I

my Aunt
Mary

Mrs. Hill

Mom, Dad,
and I

a trained
seal

the tall
man

the beach
ball

the little
boy

Mixed Addition and Subtraction

Add or subtract.

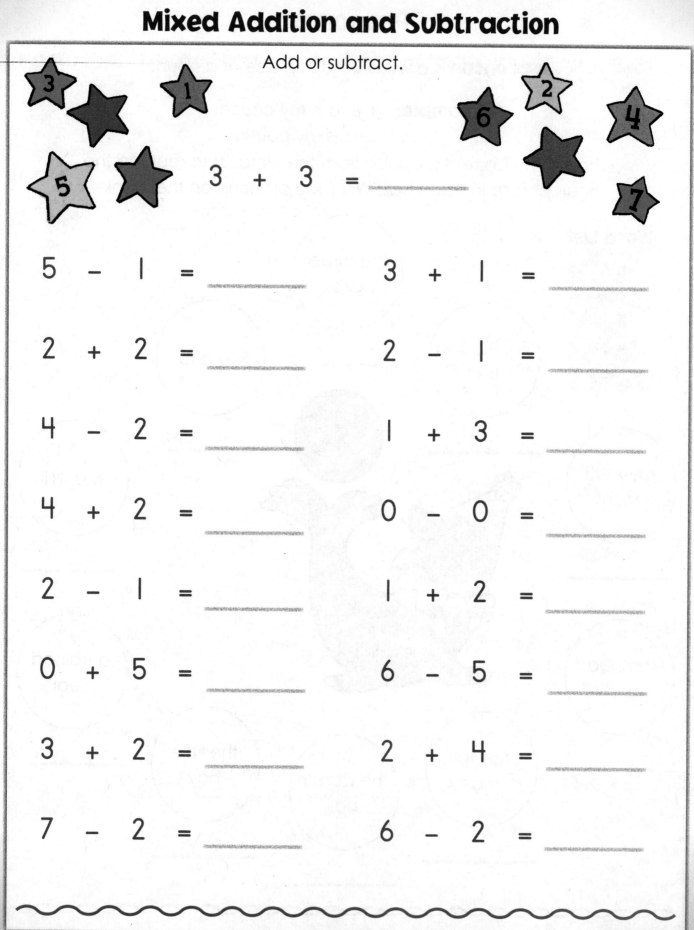

3 + 3 = _____

5 − 1 = _____   3 + 1 = _____

2 + 2 = _____   2 − 1 = _____

4 − 2 = _____   1 + 3 = _____

4 + 2 = _____   0 − 0 = _____

2 − 1 = _____   1 + 2 = _____

0 + 5 = _____   6 − 5 = _____

3 + 2 = _____   2 + 4 = _____

7 − 2 = _____   6 − 2 = _____

Short ŏ

Say the words. Listen to the short sound of the vowel **o**.

fŏx   lŏg   clŏck

Use the **ŏ** words from the word list to complete the sentences.

Word List

mop

lock

dog

My _____ is big and playful.

Let's _____ the kitchen floor.

Please _____ the door when you leave.

Write a sentence using an **ŏ** word from this page.

Creating and Reading Graphs

Ask seven friends which sport they like best.
In the box below, make a tally mark beside the sport each
one likes. Count the tally marks and color in the graph.

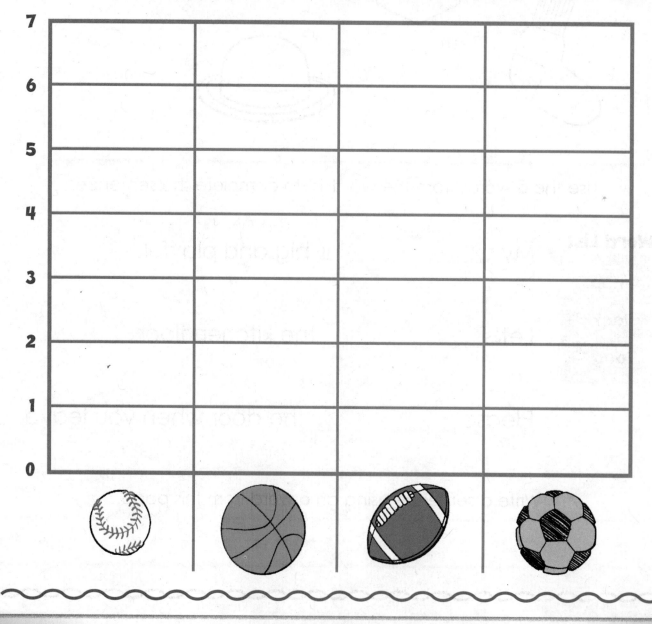

Baseball

Basketball

Football

Soccer

7

6

5

4

3

2

1

0

Singular and Plural Nouns

A noun that names one thing is called **singular**.
Examples: book, tree

A noun that names more than one thing is called **plural**.
Most words need only **s** to make them plural.
Examples: books, trees

Some words need **es** to make them plural. If a word ends with **s**, **ss**,
x, **sh**, or **ch**, add **es** to the end of the word to make it plural.
Examples: classes, churches

Circle the correct plural word.

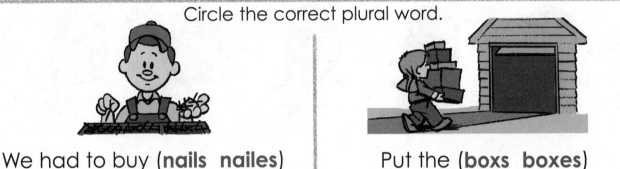

We had to buy (**nails nailes**) at the store.

Put the (**boxs boxes**) in the garage.

The (**dishs dishes**) in the sink are dirty.

We got new (**dresss dresses**) today.

The (**cooks cookes**) at this restaurant are very good.

Jerome made three (**wishs wishes**) on his birthday.

Ordinal Numbers

Use the picture below to help you match the animals in each row with the words that show their places in line.

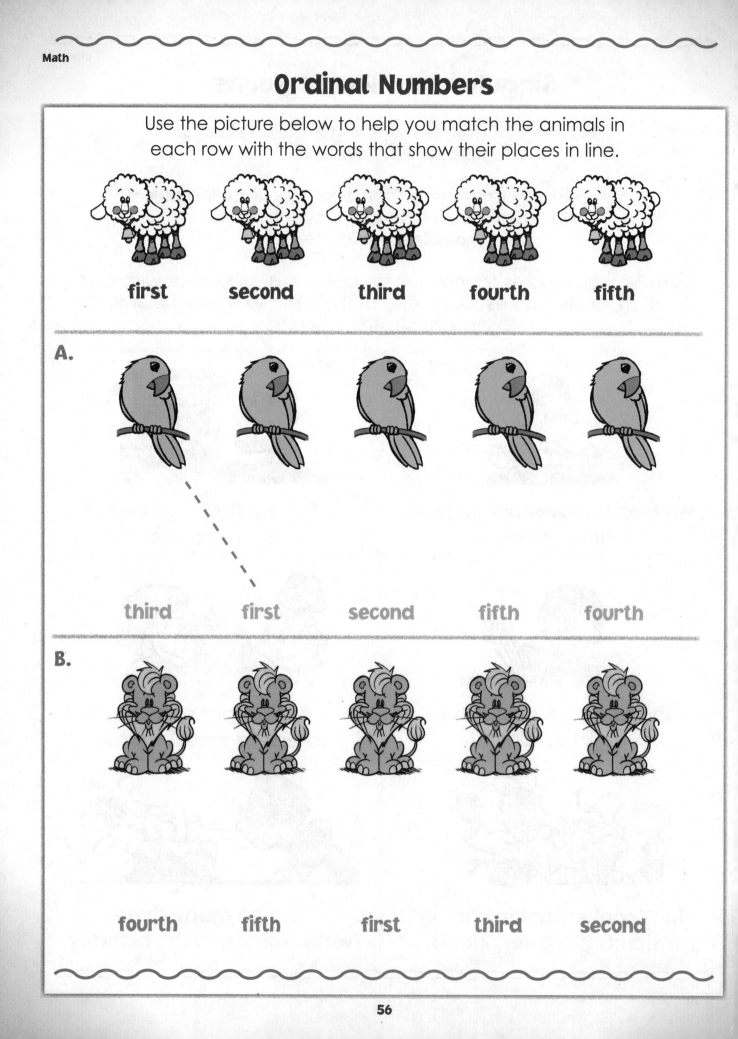

first   second   third   fourth   fifth

A.

third   first   second   fifth   fourth

B.

fourth   fifth   first   third   second

Plural Nouns (-s, -es)

Read each word. Write **s** or **es** to make the word plural.

horse_____

box_____

planet_____

wish_____

match_____

pumpkin_____

drum_____

table_____

bear_____

shell_____

brick_____

glass_____

Adding Numbers to 20

Complete each problem by writing the sum.

```
  19              8              9
 + 1            + 7            + 2
 ____           ____           ____
[    ]          [    ]          [    ]

         9              6              20
        + 5            + 6            + 0
        ____           ____           ____
        [    ]         [    ]         [    ]
```

7 + 5 = [   ]   4 + 8 = [   ]   7 + 9 = [   ]

Circle the number sentence in each pair that shows the correct sum.

9 + 2 = 11   7 + 9 = 15   0 + 20 = 20

9 + 4 = 11   7 + 8 = -15   0 + 18 = 20

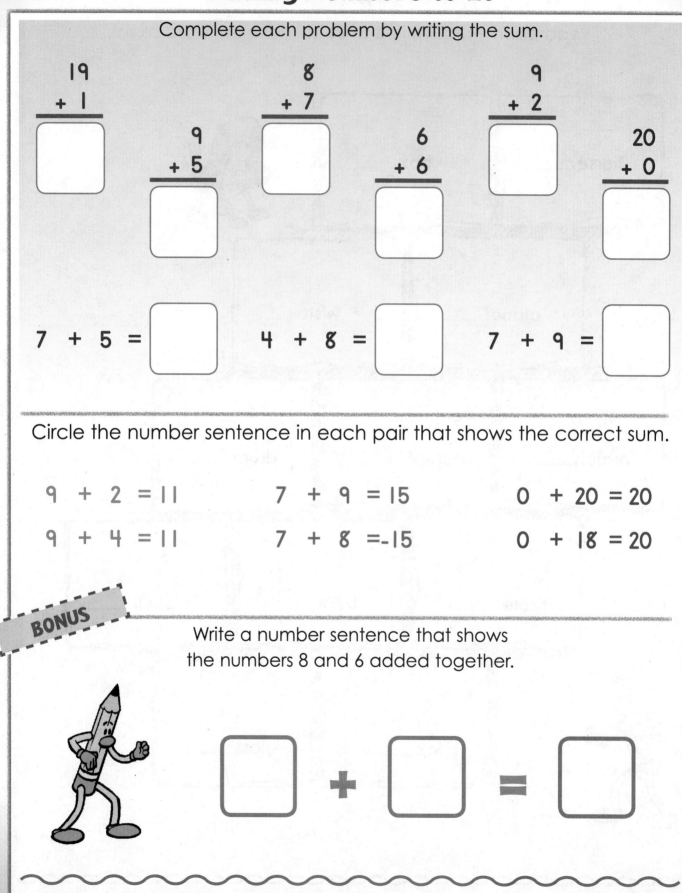

Write a number sentence that shows
the numbers 8 and 6 added together.

[   ] + [   ] = [   ]

Past Tense Verbs (-ed)

A **verb** can tell what is happening now or what has already happened (past). Most verbs add **ed** to tell the **past tense**.

Examples: **Now**   jump   I **jump** rope at recess.

              Past   jumped   I **jumped** rope yesterday.

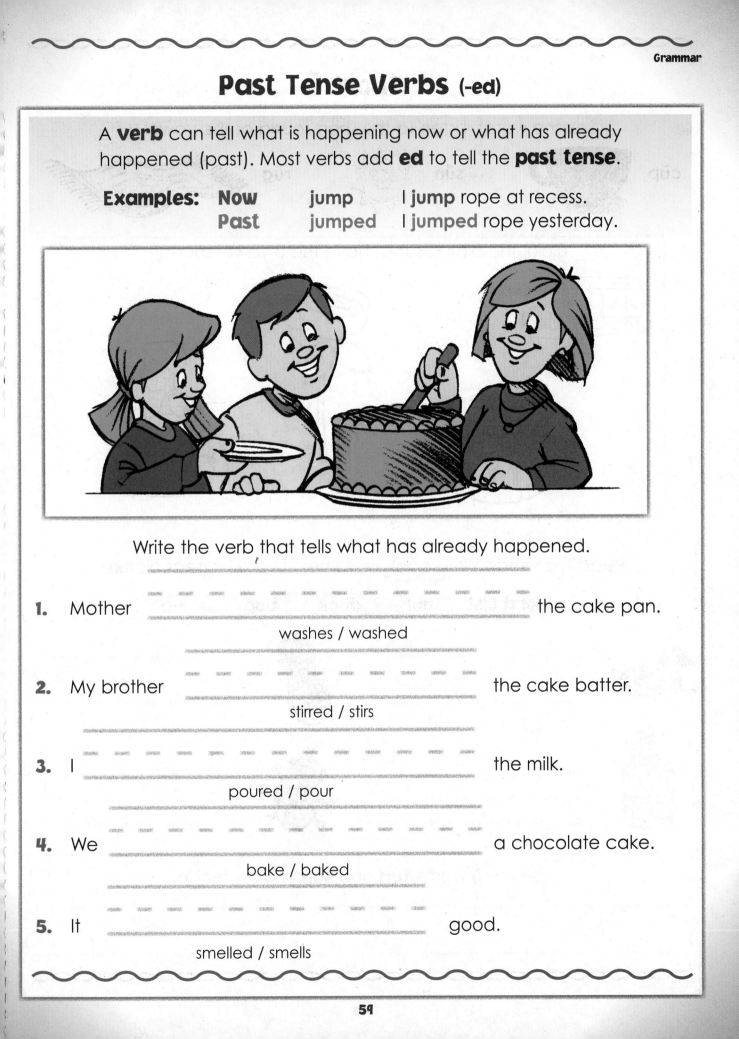

Write the verb that tells what has already happened.

1. Mother _____ the cake pan.

          washes / washed

2. My brother _____ the cake batter.

          stirred / stirs

3. I _____ the milk.

          poured / pour

4. We _____ a chocolate cake.

          bake / baked

5. It _____ good.

          smelled / smells

Short ŭ

Say the words. Listen to the short sound of the vowel **u**.

cŭp

sŭn

rŭg

Color the pictures that have the ŭ vowel sound.

Read the words. Write each word next to the correct picture.

Word List   nut   duck   bug   jug

Use the ŭ words **fun** and **sun** in a sentence.

Story Problems

Write a number sentence to solve each story problem.

Example: David wrote **14** letters.
Terry wrote **5** letters.
How many letters did they write altogether?

14	+	5	=	19
(number of letters David wrote)		(number of letters Terry wrote)		(total number of letters written)

A. Anthony held **7** rocks in one hand.
He held **9** rocks in his other hand.
What was the total number of rocks he held?

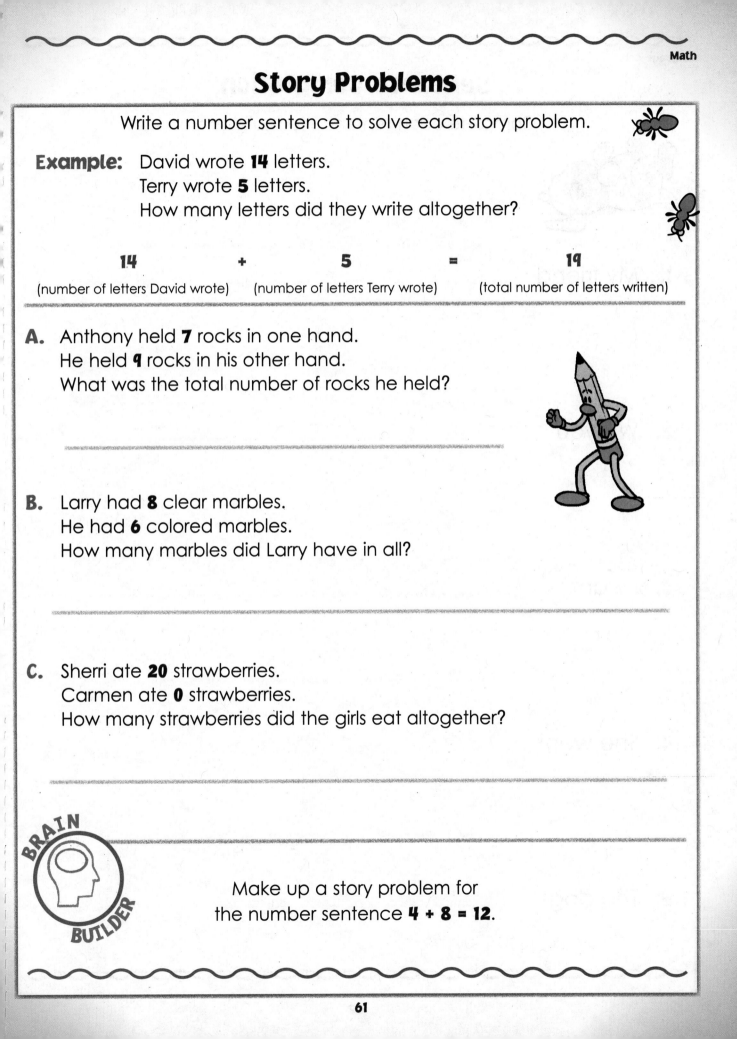

B. Larry had **8** clear marbles.
He had **6** colored marbles.
How many marbles did Larry have in all?

C. Sherri ate **20** strawberries.
Carmen ate **0** strawberries.
How many strawberries did the girls eat altogether?

BRAIN BUILDER

Make up a story problem for
the number sentence **4 + 8 = 12**.

Sentence Completion

Complete each sentence to make sense.

1. My friend _____ .

2. Will you _____ ?

3. I want _____ .

4. She went _____ .

5. The dogs _____ .

Subtraction to 20

Subtract.

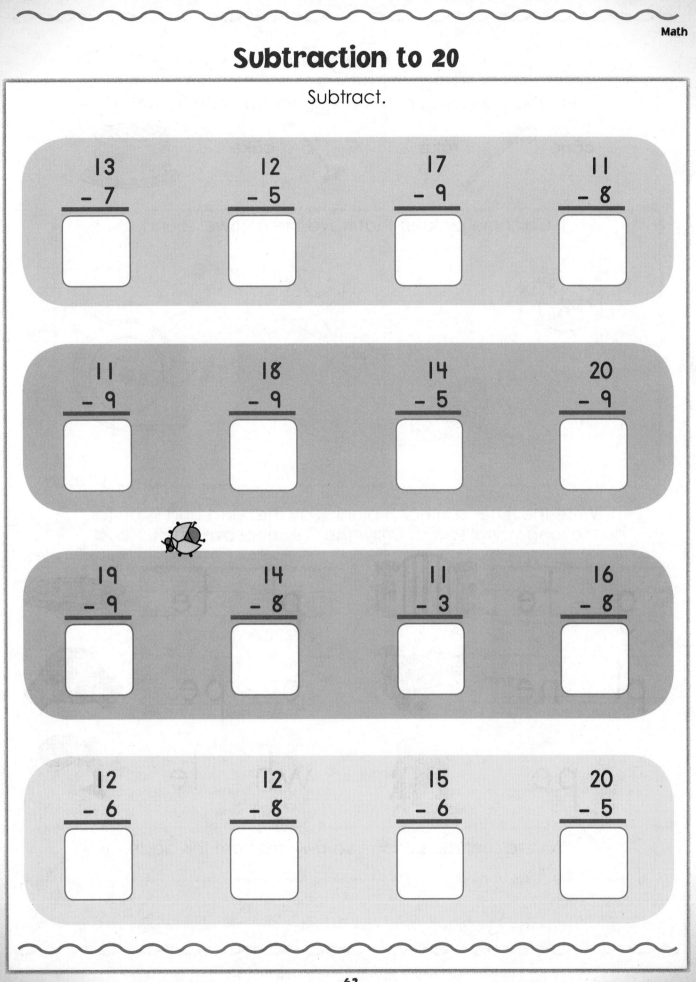

13 − 7	12 − 5	17 − 9	11 − 8
11 − 9	18 − 9	14 − 5	20 − 9
19 − 9	14 − 8	11 − 3	16 − 8
12 − 6	12 − 8	15 − 6	20 − 5

Long ā

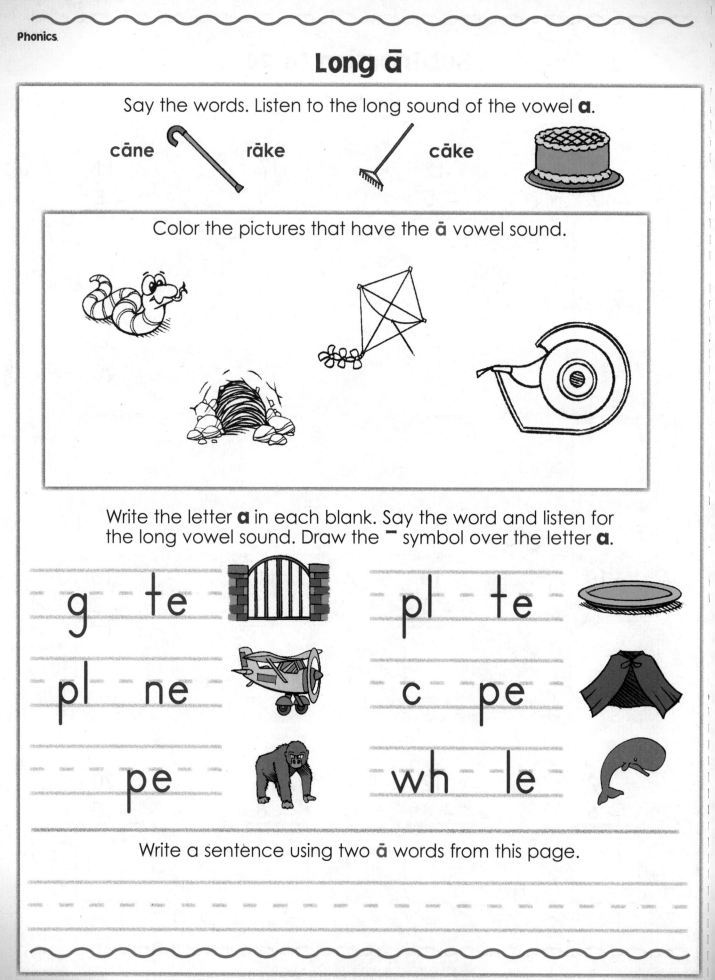

Say the words. Listen to the long sound of the vowel **a**.

cāne   rāke   cāke

Color the pictures that have the **ā** vowel sound.

Write the letter **a** in each blank. Say the word and listen for the long vowel sound. Draw the ⁻ symbol over the letter **a**.

g te   pl te

pl ne   c pe

pe   wh le

Write a sentence using two **ā** words from this page.

Cut and paste these words in "My Big Book of Words,"
found on pages 67–70. Put them in alphabetical order.

(Write your
own words.)

ant	get	make	stop	
apple	goat	maybe	swim	
ball	gone	mine	tent	
balloon	happy	nest	there	
can	have	nose	under	
cat	hide	on	up	
come	inside	open	vase	
dark	it	pig	very	
dig	joke	play	wagon	
dog	jump	pretty	want	
eat	key	quill	work	
egg	kite	quit	xylophone	
end	kitten	rabbit	yak	
fish	lamp	red	yellow	
four	like	run	zipper	
fox	look	said	zoo	

Remove pages 67–70. Cut along dashed lines. Staple pages in order.

My Big Book of Words

Write in your own words or use the
"cut-and-paste" words found on page 65.
Put the words in alphabetical order.

1

Ee	Ff	Gg	Hh

3

Aa | Bb | Cc | Dd

Ii | Jj | Kk | Ll

2

4

Mm | Nn | Oo | Pp

Uu | Vv | Ww | Xx

5

7

Qq | Rr | Ss | Tt

6

Yy | Zz | My Favorite Words

8

Fact Families

A fact family is a group of addition and subtraction number sentences that have the same three numbers.

9 + 8 = 17		17 - 9 = 8	
8 + 9 = 17		17 - 8 = 9	

The numbers 8, 9, and 17 are used in the **fact family** above.

Complete each number sentence. Draw a line to match each pair of number sentences from the same fact family.

8 + 7 = ☐   3 + 9 = ☐

9 + 3 = ☐   7 + 8 = ☐

6 + 5 = ☐   7 + 9 = ☐

9 + 7 = ☐   5 + 6 = ☐

Write two addition number sentences to complete each fact family. Use the same three numbers as in the subtraction number sentences.

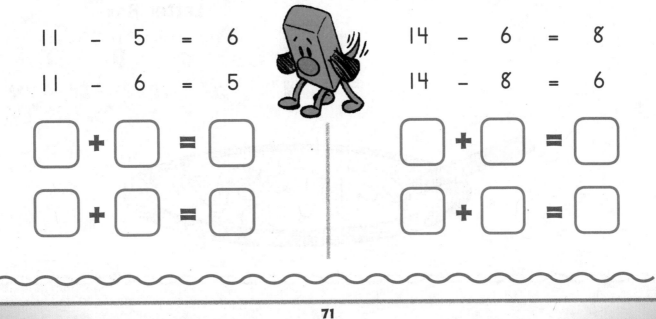

11 - 5 = 6   14 - 6 = 8

11 - 6 = 5   14 - 8 = 6

☐ + ☐ = ☐   ☐ + ☐ = ☐

☐ + ☐ = ☐   ☐ + ☐ = ☐

Rhyming Words

See how many words you can print that rhyme with **man**. First, try to add different letters to **-an** on your own. Use the letter box if you get stuck.

1.

2.

3.

4.

5.

6.

7.

8.

9.

Letter Box

b   c   D   f

N   p   r   t   v

Missing Addends

In some number sentences, an addend is missing.

$$6 + \boxed{} = 13$$

To solve, think . . . "6 plus **how many** equals 13?"

$$6 + \boxed{7} = 13$$

$$6 + \boxed{} = 12 \qquad 7 + \boxed{} = 12$$

$$19 + \boxed{} = 20 \qquad 2 + \boxed{} = 11$$

$$1 + \boxed{} = 15 \qquad 8 + \boxed{} = 11$$

$$\begin{array}{r} 4 \\ + \boxed{} \\ \hline 13 \end{array}$$

$$\begin{array}{r} 5 \\ \boxed{} \\ + \\ \hline 13 \end{array}$$

$$\begin{array}{r} 7 \\ + \boxed{} \\ \hline 14 \end{array} \qquad \begin{array}{r} 3 \\ + \boxed{} \\ \hline 12 \end{array} \qquad \begin{array}{r} 9 \\ + \boxed{} \\ \hline 18 \end{array}$$

Make up two problems of your own.

$$\boxed{} + \boxed{} = \boxed{12} \qquad \boxed{} + \boxed{} = \boxed{10}$$

Long ē

Say the words. Listen to the long sound of the vowel **e**.

scēne   thēse   ēve

Read each word in the word list.
Use the words to complete each sentence.
Draw the ▬ symbol above the long vowel sound.

Word List   Steve   even   scene   Eve

1. The boy's name is _____ .

2. We watched the first _____ of the play.

3. We have a special dinner on Christmas _____ .

4. The teacher asked me to name an _____ number.

Write your own sentence using one ē word from the word list.

_____

_____

Doubles Facts

Sometimes a number is added to itself.
These number sentences are called **doubles facts**.

$$5 + 5 = 10 \qquad 8 + 8 = 16$$

Complete the doubles facts.

7 + 7 = ☐

2 + ☐ = 4

5 + ☐ = 10

4 + 4 = ☐

10 + 10 = ☐

9 + ☐ = 18

1 + ☐ = 2

☐ + 4 = 8

7 + ☐ = 14

3 + 3 = ☐

0 + 0 = ☐

5 + 5 = ☐

6 + 6 = ☐

1 + 1 = ☐

```
   ☐
 + 3
 ───
   6
```

```
   8
 + 8
 ───
   ☐
```

```
   ☐
 + 6
 ───
  12
```

Action Words

Complete each sentence.

Word List

swing	jump	walk
run	ride	swim

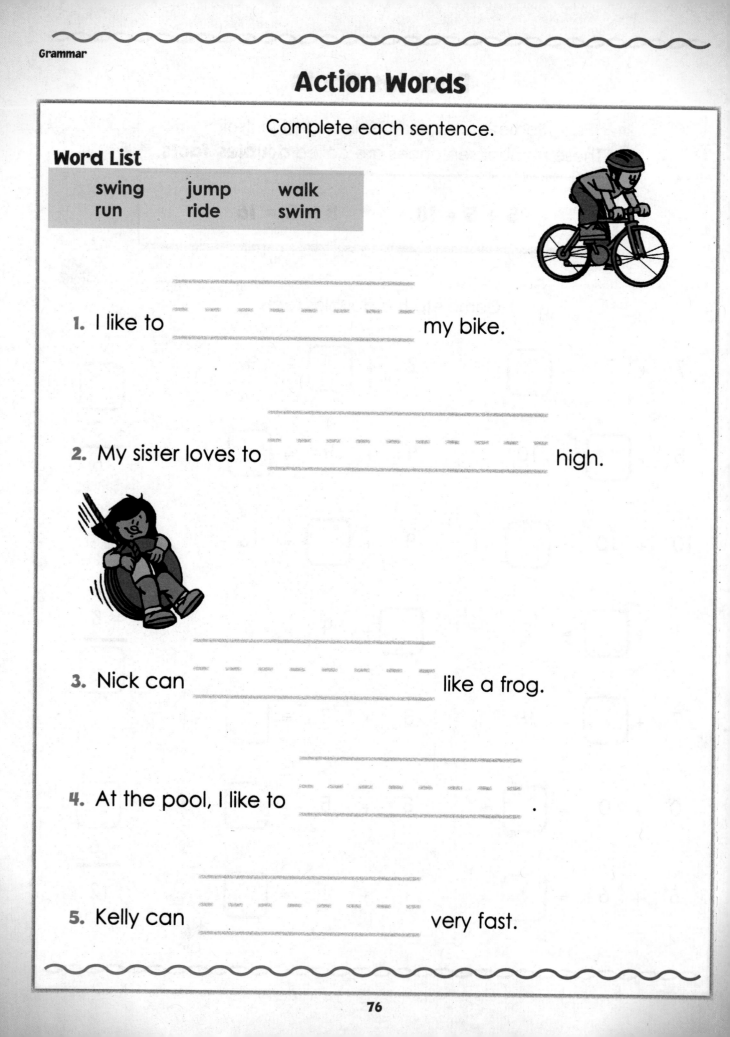

1. I like to _____ my bike.

2. My sister loves to _____ high.

3. Nick can _____ like a frog.

4. At the pool, I like to _____.

5. Kelly can _____ very fast.

Rhyming Pairs

Fill in the blank with a word that rhymes with the word in color.

She likes to **run** under the _____ .

I see a **bee** up in the _____ .

He can **hop** over the _____ .

There is a **man** inside the _____ .

BRAIN BUILDER

Make up a rhyme.
Draw a picture of your rhyme on another sheet of paper.

Tens and Ones

Write the number that each drawing represents.

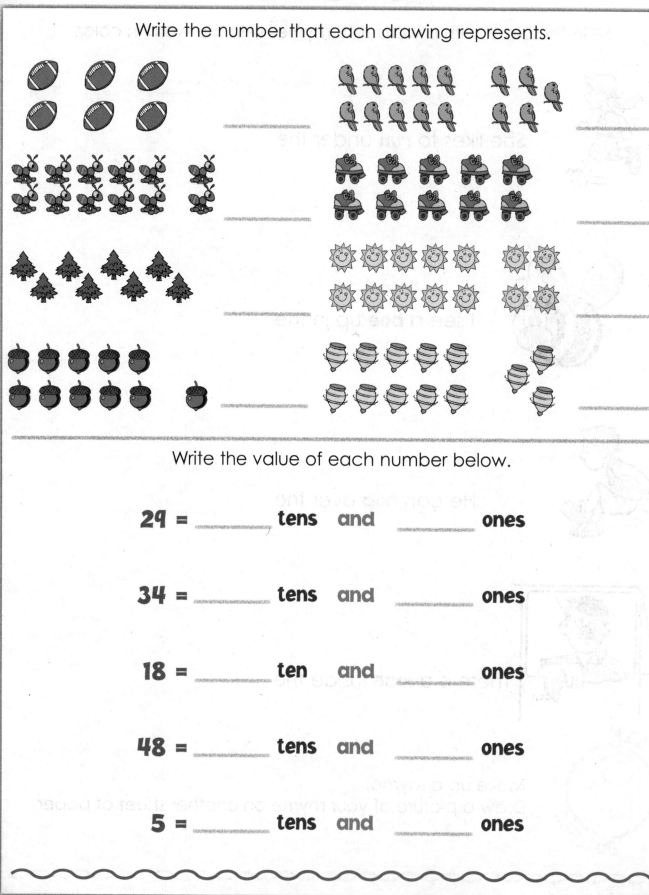

Write the value of each number below.

29 = _____ **tens** and _____ **ones**

34 = _____ **tens** and _____ **ones**

18 = _____ **ten** and _____ **ones**

48 = _____ **tens** and _____ **ones**

5 = _____ **tens** and _____ **ones**

Punctuation Marks

Write the correct **punctuation mark** at the end
of each sentence. Put a **?** or **.** in each box.

1. Have you been to the circus ☐

2. We went on Saturday ☐

3. We saw monkeys ☐

4. Would you like to be a clown ☐

5. We ate lots of fluffy, pink cotton candy ☐

6. Have you ever had a candy apple ☐

7. It is my favorite thing to eat ☐

Place Value Practice

Write the number of tens and ones.

	tens	ones
20 =		

	tens	ones
16 =		

	tens	ones
14 =		

	tens	ones
31 =		

	tens	ones
22 =		

	tens	ones
12 =		

	tens	ones
47 =		

	tens	ones
24 =		

	tens	ones
36 =		

	tens	ones
55 =		

	tens	ones
11 =		

	tens	ones
63 =		

	tens	ones
21 =		

	tens	ones
17 =		

	tens	ones
69 =		

BRAIN BUILDER

Add these numbers: **41, 26, 11**.
How many tens and ones
are in your answer?

tens	ones

Long ī

Say the words. Listen to the long sound of the vowel **i**.

kīte   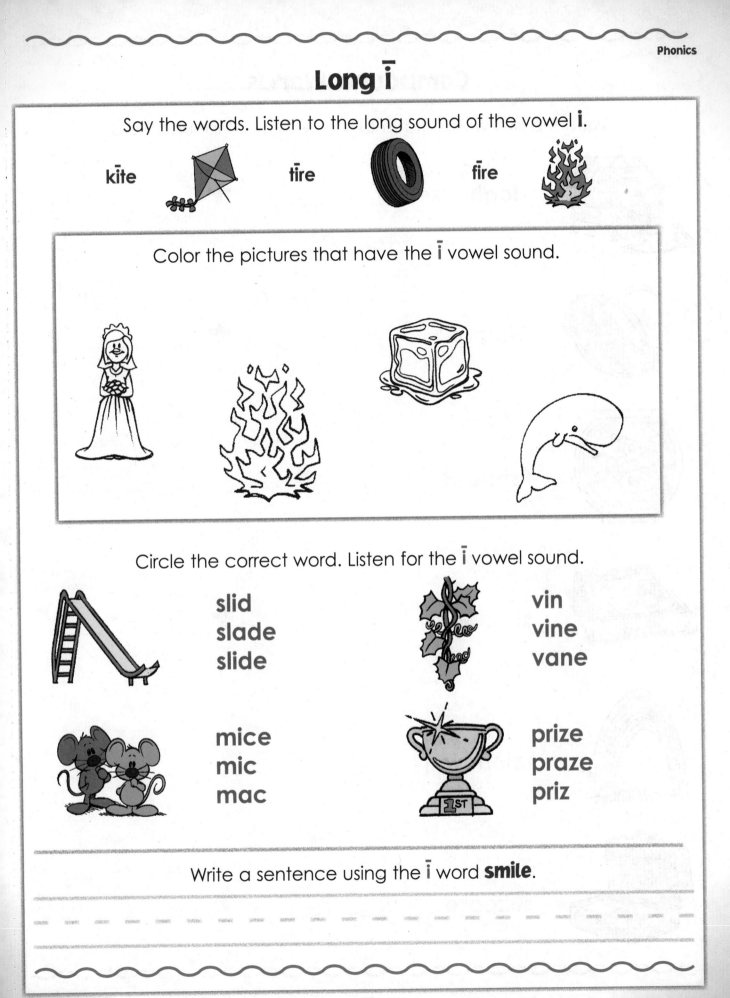   tīre   fīre

Color the pictures that have the ī vowel sound.

Circle the correct word. Listen for the ī vowel sound.

slid
slade
slide

vin
vine
vane

mice
mic
mac

prize
praze
priz

Write a sentence using the ī word **smile**.

Compound Words

Write the two words that make up each compound word.

doghouse _____ + _____

football _____ + _____

fishbowl _____ + _____

sandbox _____ + _____

rainbow _____ + _____

suitcase _____ + _____

Adding Two-Digit Numbers

Add the tens and ones to find the two-digit sum.

2 tens and **6** ones
+ 1 ten and **3** ones

  3 tens and 9 ones **=** 39

1 ten and **4** ones
+ 3 tens and **3** ones

☐ tens and ☐ ones **=**

1 ten and **3** ones
+ 1 ten and **1** one

☐ tens and ☐ ones **=**

2 tens and **5** ones
+ 2 tens and **0** ones

☐ tens and ☐ ones **=**

1 ten and **6** ones
+ 2 tens and **3** ones

☐ tens and ☐ ones **=**

1 ten and **4** ones
+ 3 tens and **1** one

☐ tens and ☐ ones **=**

1 ten and **5** ones
+ 2 tens and **4** ones

☐ tens and ☐ ones **=**

2 tens and **3** ones
+ 2 tens and **2** ones

☐ tens and ☐ ones **=**

3 tens and **2** ones
+ 1 ten and **1** one

☐ tens and ☐ ones **=**

3 tens and **7** ones
+ 1 ten and **2** ones

☐ tens and ☐ ones **=**

Two Words in One

Write the two words that make each compound word.

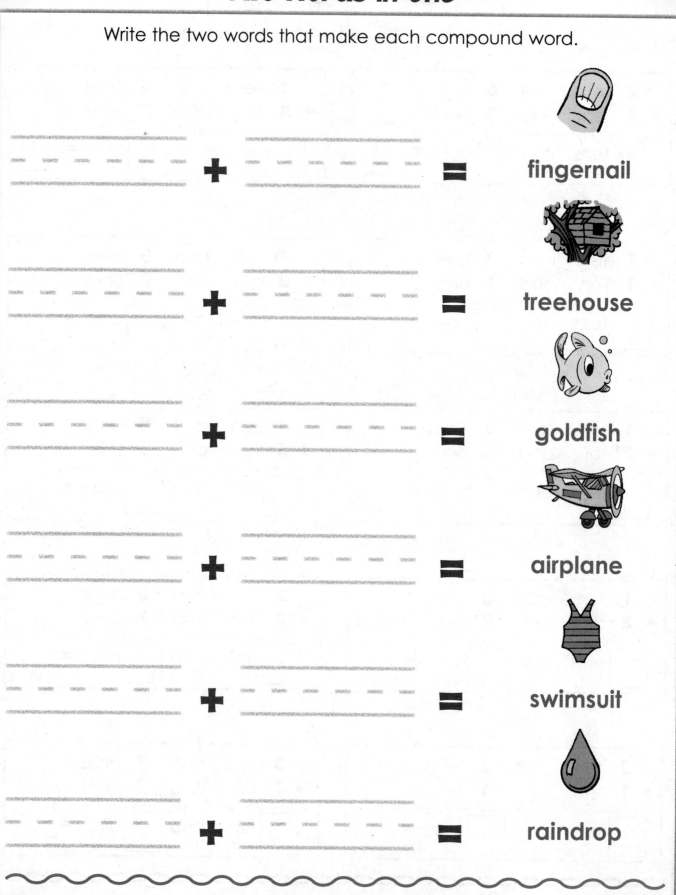

_____ + _____ = **fingernail**

_____ + _____ = **treehouse**

_____ + _____ = **goldfish**

_____ + _____ = **airplane**

_____ + _____ = **swimsuit**

_____ + _____ = **raindrop**

Double-Digit Addition

Add. Color the spaces with sums **greater** than 50 red.
Color the spaces with sums **less** than 50 blue.

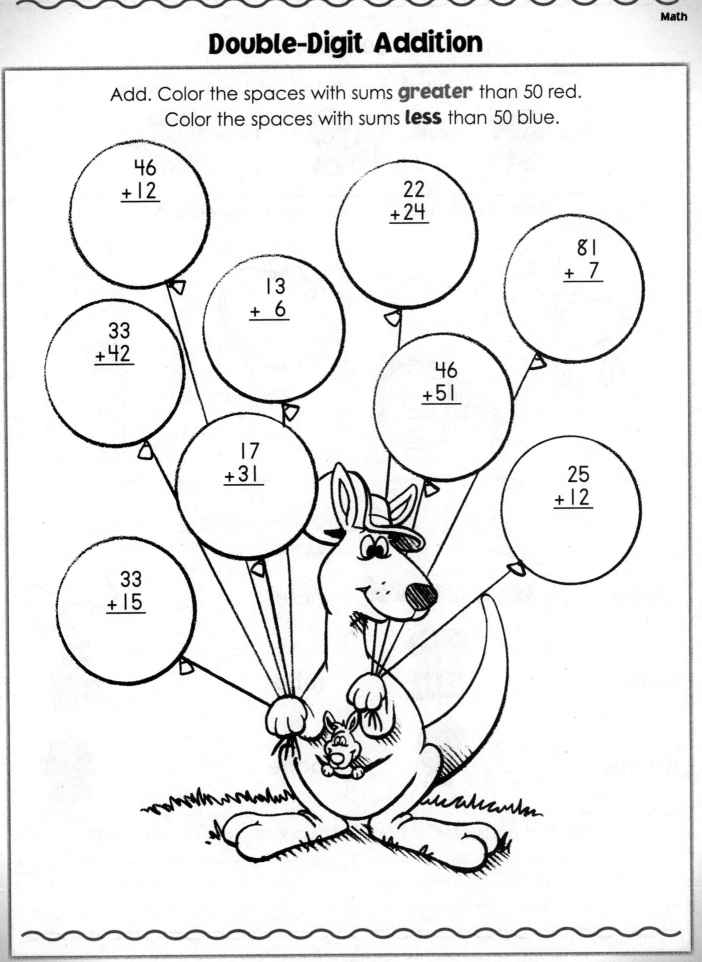

$$\begin{array}{r} 46 \\ +12 \\ \hline \end{array}$$

$$\begin{array}{r} 22 \\ +24 \\ \hline \end{array}$$

$$\begin{array}{r} 81 \\ +\ 7 \\ \hline \end{array}$$

$$\begin{array}{r} 13 \\ +\ 6 \\ \hline \end{array}$$

$$\begin{array}{r} 33 \\ +42 \\ \hline \end{array}$$

$$\begin{array}{r} 46 \\ +51 \\ \hline \end{array}$$

$$\begin{array}{r} 17 \\ +31 \\ \hline \end{array}$$

$$\begin{array}{r} 25 \\ +12 \\ \hline \end{array}$$

$$\begin{array}{r} 33 \\ +15 \\ \hline \end{array}$$

Long ō

Say the words. Listen to the long sound of the vowel **o**.

rōse   vōte   nōse

Color the pictures that have the **ō** vowel sound.

Match each word to the correct picture.
Draw the ‾ symbol above the long vowel.

globe

rope

phone

note

robe

bone

What two parts of your body have names with the **ō** sound?

86

Connect the Sums

Add. Connect the equal sums. Color the picture.

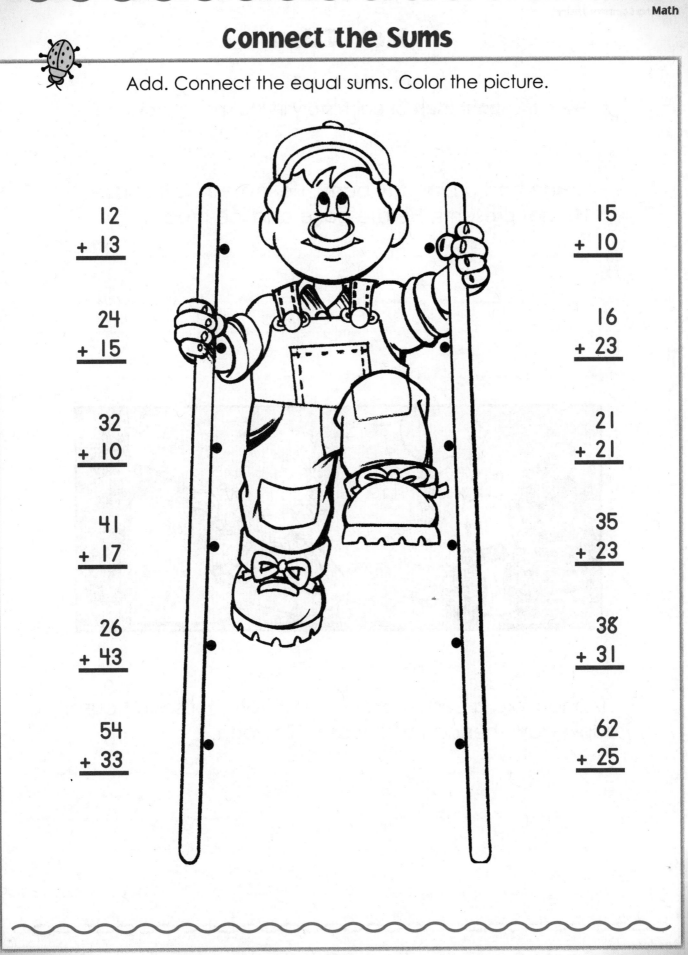

12
+ 13

24
+ 15

32
+ 10

41
+ 17

26
+ 43

54
+ 33

15
+ 10

16
+ 23

21
+ 21

35
+ 23

38
+ 31

62
+ 25

Main Idea

Read the stories below.
Write the **main idea** of each story in the space provided.

Joe had a birthday party. He invited his friends.
He got presents. He ate cake and ice cream.

Teena wore a costume. She went from house to house.
People gave her candy. It was Halloween.

Astro-Addition

Find the sums. Color the picture.

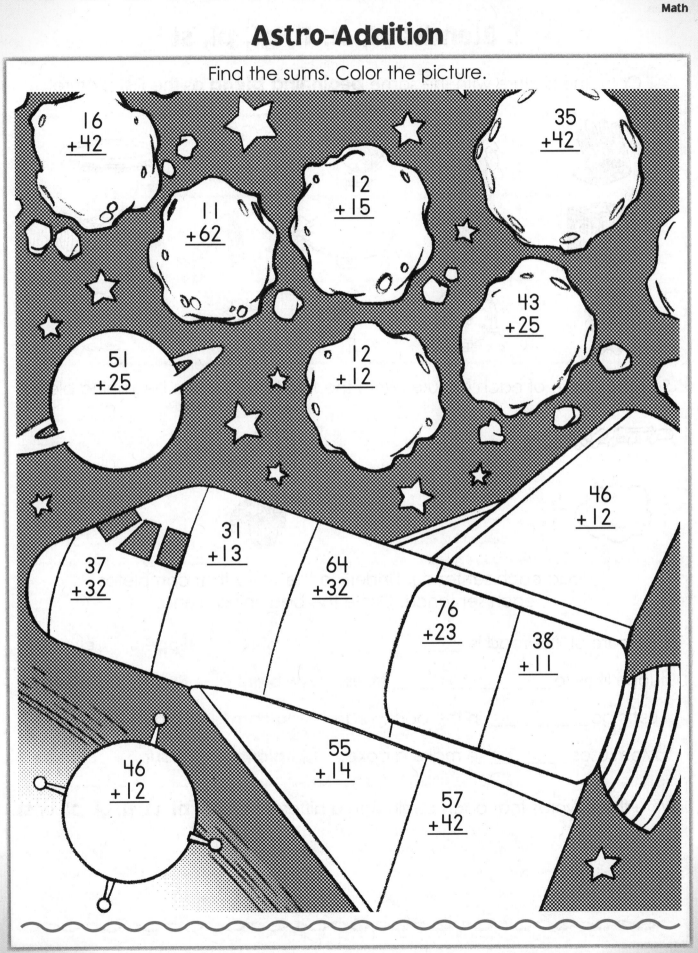

L Blends: bl, cl, fl, gl, pl, sl

Color the picture with the same **beginning blend** as the first picture.

Say the name of each picture. Write the two letters of the beginning blend.

Read each sentence. Underline the word that completes
each sentence. Circle the beginning blend.

Be careful, the road is _____ .	glue	slippery	cloudy
John likes to _____ trees.	blare	flower	climb
Let's go _____ in the backyard.	gloom	play	blue
Mom uses _____ to make a cake.	plants	flour	clothes

Write three words that each begin with a different blend: **bl, cl, fl, gl, pl,** or **sl.**

Number Words

Count the dots above each line. Print the correct number word.

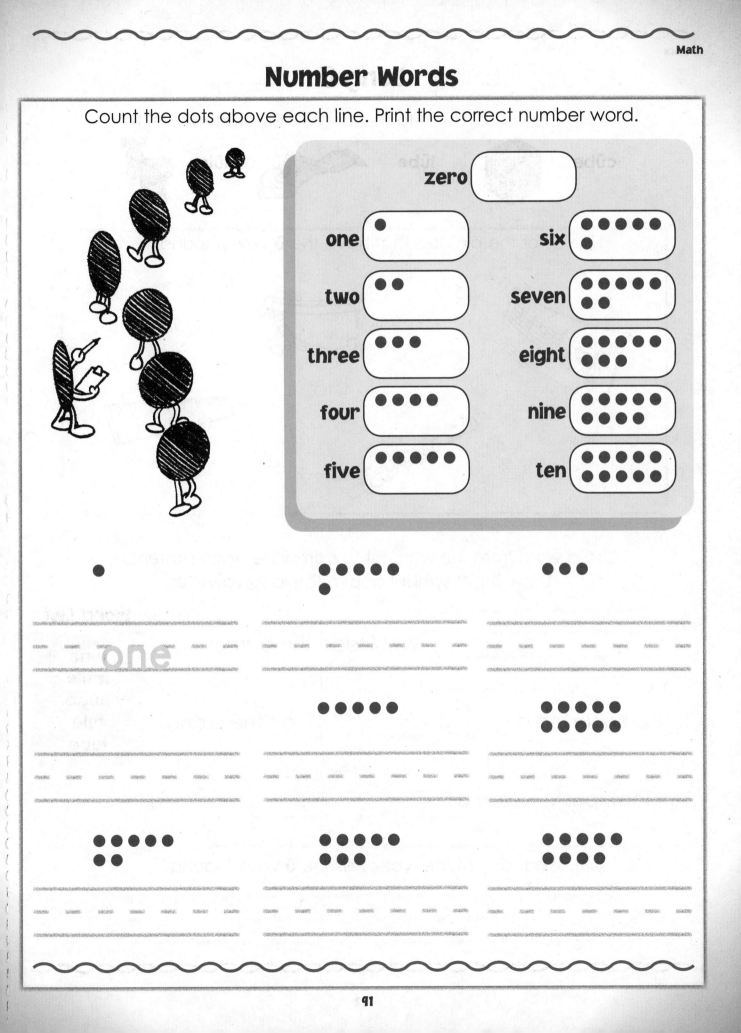

zero

one •

two • •

three • • •

four • • • •

five • • • • •

six • • • • • •

seven • • • • • • •

eight • • • • • • •

nine • • • • • • • • •

ten • • • • • • • • • •

one

Long Ū

Say the words. Listen to the long sound of the vowel **u**.

cūbe   tūbe   mūle

Color the pictures that have the **ū** vowel sound.

Use a word from the word list to complete each sentence.
Draw the ¯ symbol above the long vowel **u**.

The _____ was inside the barn.

The boy played a _____ on the piano.

The toothpaste was in a _____ .

Word List

tune
mule
huge
rule
tube

What day of the week has the **ū** vowel sound?

_____

_____

Remove pages 93–96. Cut along dashed lines. Staple pages in order.

My First Crossword Puzzle Book

Use the word list to solve the crossword puzzle.

Word List

cake
games
ice
gift

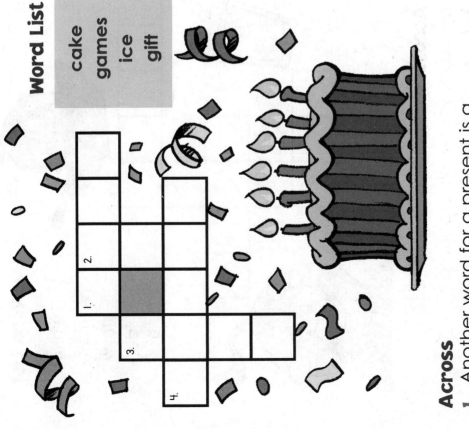

Across
1. Another word for a present is a _____.
4. We played lots of _____ at the party.

Down
2. We had cake and _____ cream.
3. There were many candles on the _____.

Use the word list to solve the crossword puzzle.

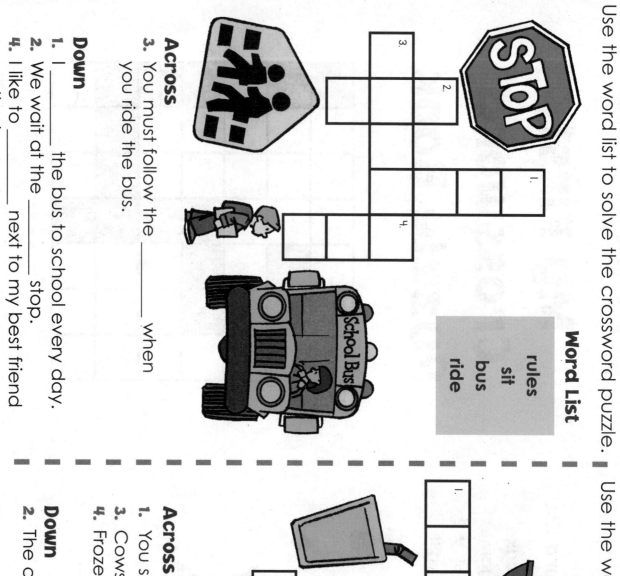

Word List

rules
sit
bus
ride

Across

3. You must follow the _____ when you ride the bus.

Down

1. I _____ the bus to school every day.
2. We wait at the _____ stop.
4. I like to _____ next to my best friend on the bus.

2

Use the word list to solve the crossword puzzle.

Word List

white
milk
straw
ice

Across

1. You sip your drink through a _____ to drink.
3. Cows give us _____.
4. Frozen water is called _____.

Down

2. The color of vanilla ice cream is _____.

4

Use the word list to solve the crossword puzzle.

Word List

save
pigs
dime
bank

Across

2. Keep your money in a ____.
4. A 10¢ coin is a ____.

Down

1. My bank helps me ____ money.
3. Many coin banks look like ____.

Use the word list to solve the crossword puzzle.

Word List

fly
park
tail
year

Across

2. I fly my kite in the ____.
3. Kites, birds, and airplanes can ____.

Down

1. The ____ is at the end of a kite.
4. Spring is the best time of ____ to fly a kite.

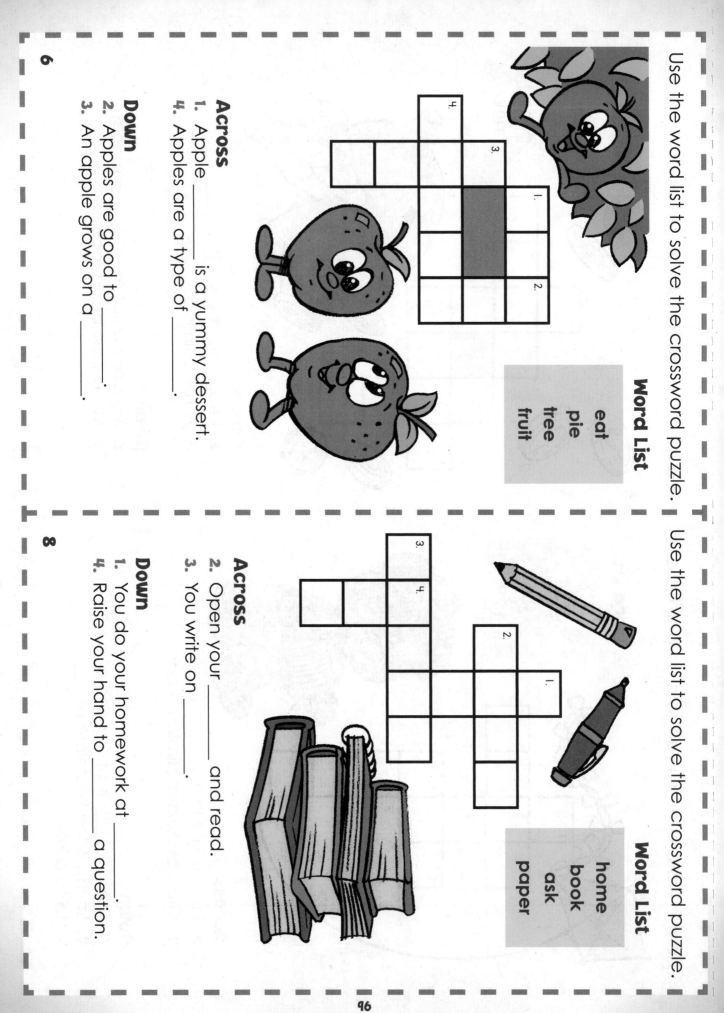

Use the word list to solve the crossword puzzle.

Word List

eat
pie
tree
fruit

Across

1. Apple _____ is a yummy dessert.
4. Apples are a type of _____.

Down

2. Apples are good to _____.
3. An apple grows on a _____.

6

Use the word list to solve the crossword puzzle.

Word List

home
book
ask
paper

Across

2. Open your _____ and read.
3. You write on _____.

Down

1. You do your homework at _____.
4. Raise your hand to _____ a question.

8

R Blends: br, cr, dr, fr, gr, pr, tr

Circle the blend at the beginning of each word. Say the word.

1. proud	2. brain	3. dress	4. crest
5. greet	6. track	7. free	8. drag
9. trampoline	10. crack	11. pretend	12. bring
13. dream	14. brown	15. groom	16. frozen

Say the name of each picture.
Circle the blend you hear at the beginning of the word.

pr fr cr	gr tr cr	cr fr pr
fr gr tr	gr dr br	tr pr cr

Say the name of each picture. Write the two letters of the beginning blend.

Calendar Questions

Write the name of the month. Fill in the numbers of the days.

Month:

Sunday	Monday	Tuesday	Wednesday	Thursday	Friday	Saturday

A. How many days in one week? _____

B. How many days in this month? _____

C. How many months in a year? _____

D. How many seasons in a year? _____

E. What is your favorite season? _____

Let's Shop!

Look at each box. Circle the item you can buy.

How Much Money?

Write the value of the coins shown on each hat.
Color the hat with the greatest value.

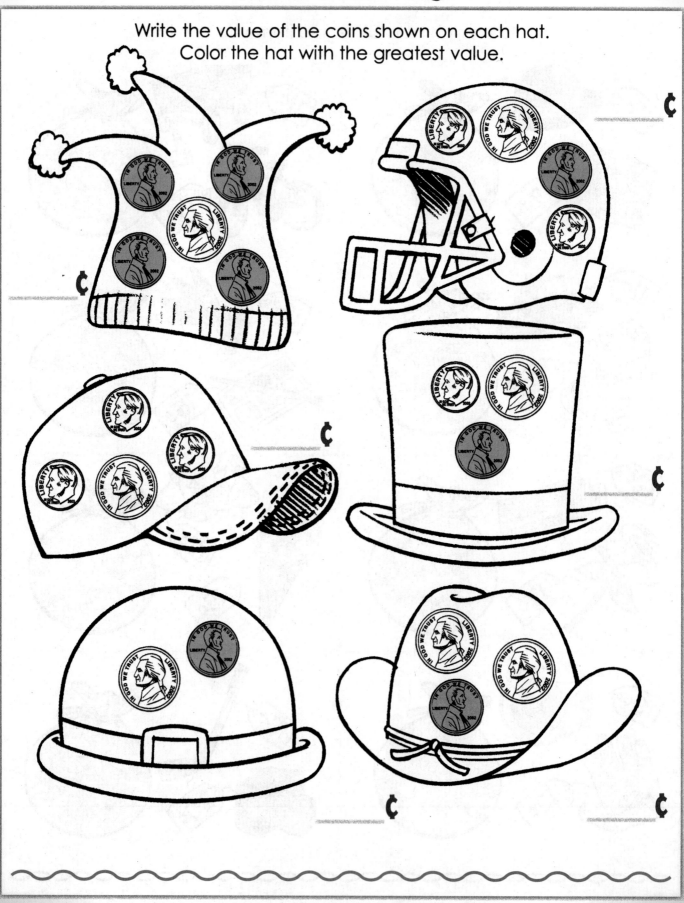

Greater Than or Less Than?

Circle the number that is **larger** >.

2 or (7)

33 or 22   27 or 72

9 or 21   24 or 15

44 or 51

103 or 100

Circle the number that is **smaller** <.

5 or (2)

64 or 72

104 or 102

27 or 41

46 or 26

17 or 37

15 or 51

80 or 8

Beginning Blends: sk, sm, sn, sp, st, sw, tw

Color the picture with the same **beginning blend** as the first picture.

Circle the blend at the beginning of each word. Say the word.

1. ski   **2.** twenty   **3.** smother   **4.** stare   **5.** tweezer

6. sting   **7.** smog   **8.** sneeze   **9.** spend   **10.** swat

Write the word from the word list that completes
each sentence. Circle the beginning blend.

Word List

sky
twins
stamp
snow

I need a _____ to mail my letter.

Jill and Bill are _____ .

Let's go sledding in the _____ .

Look at the clouds in the _____ !

Counting Money

Count the coins on each box. Write the value on the line.

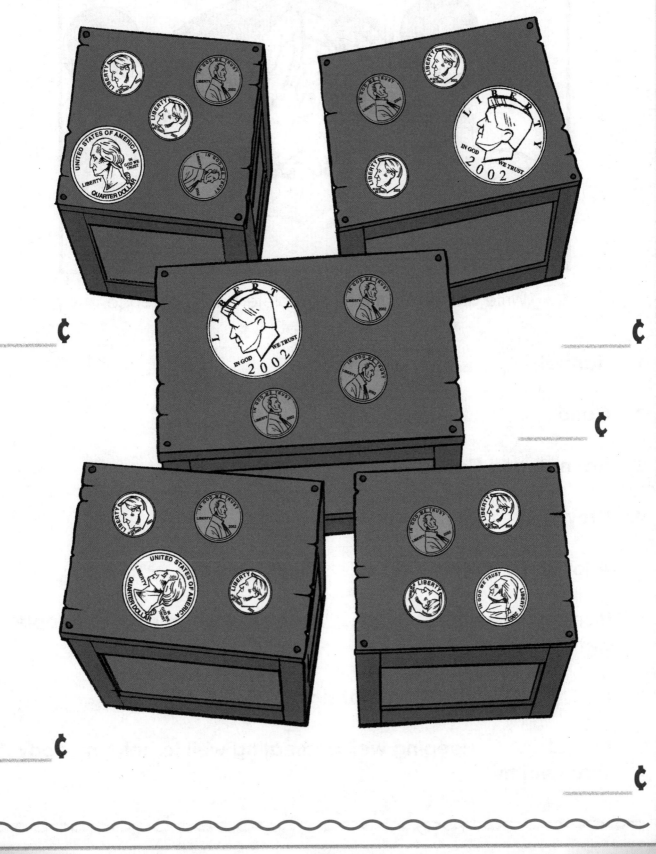

¢

¢

¢

¢

¢

103

Linking Verbs: am, is, are

Write **am**, **is**, or **are** to complete each sentence.

1. Hannah _____ sick today.

2. Carlos _____ sick, too.

3. Hannah and Carlos _____ not in school.

4. They _____ at home resting.

5. A lot of my friends _____ getting sick.

6. It seems like winter _____ a time when a lot of people get sick.

7. I _____ glad I am not sick.

8. I _____ sleeping well and eating well to help my body stay healthy.

Measuring in Inches

Look at each ruler.
Write the length of each object in **inches**.

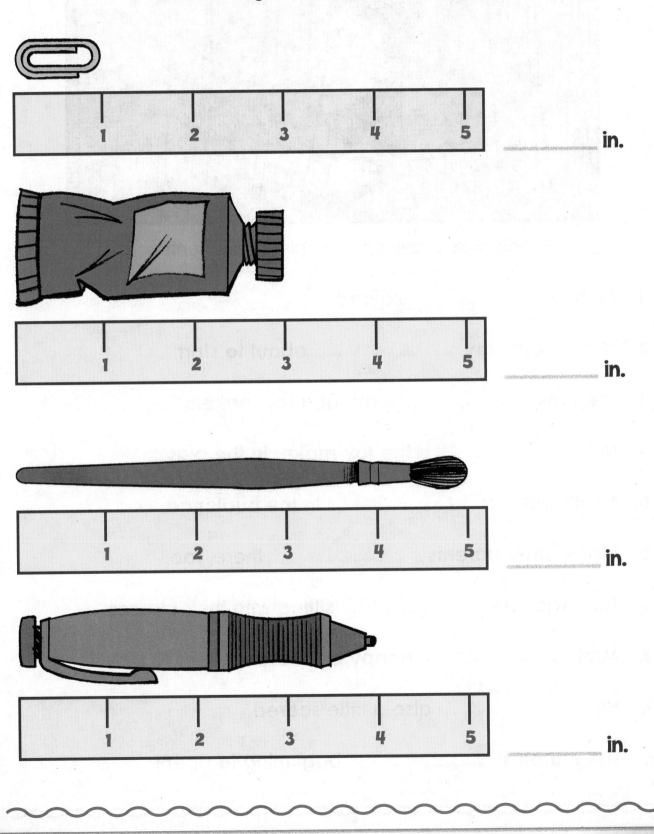

_____ in.

_____ in.

_____ in.

_____ in.

Linking Verbs: was, were

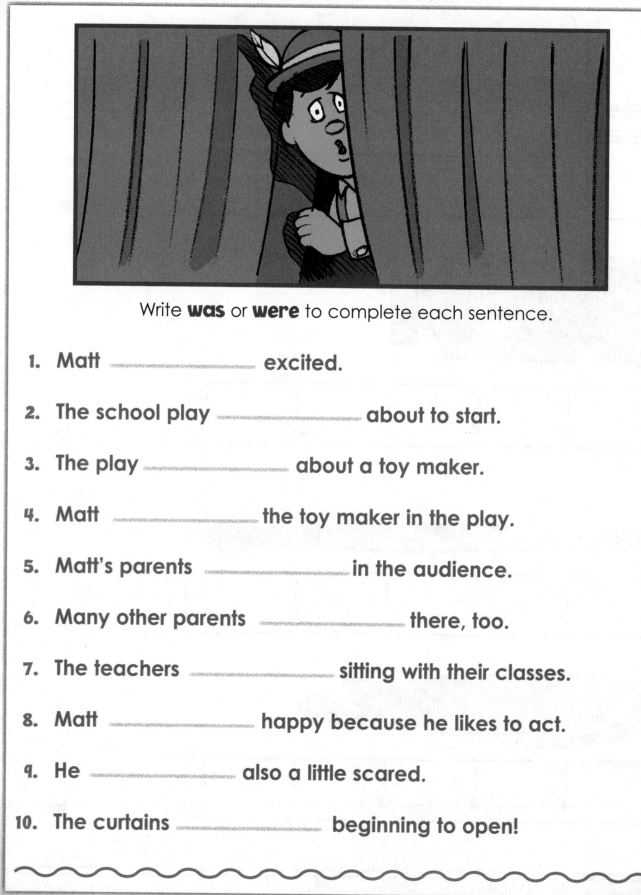

Write **was** or **were** to complete each sentence.

1. Matt _____ excited.

2. The school play _____ about to start.

3. The play _____ about a toy maker.

4. Matt _____ the toy maker in the play.

5. Matt's parents _____ in the audience.

6. Many other parents _____ there, too.

7. The teachers _____ sitting with their classes.

8. Matt _____ happy because he likes to act.

9. He _____ also a little scared.

10. The curtains _____ beginning to open!

Time on the Hour

The short hand shows the **hour**.
The long hand shows the **minutes**.

**The time on this clock is
3:00 or 3 o'clock.**

Write the time on the lines.

_____ : _____ o'clock   _____ : _____ o'clock   _____ : _____ o'clock   _____ : _____ o'clock

_____ : _____ o'clock   _____ : _____ o'clock   _____ : _____ o'clock   _____ : _____ o'clock

Two-Digit Subtraction

Subtract the numbers to find the differences.
Draw a line between the answers that are the same.

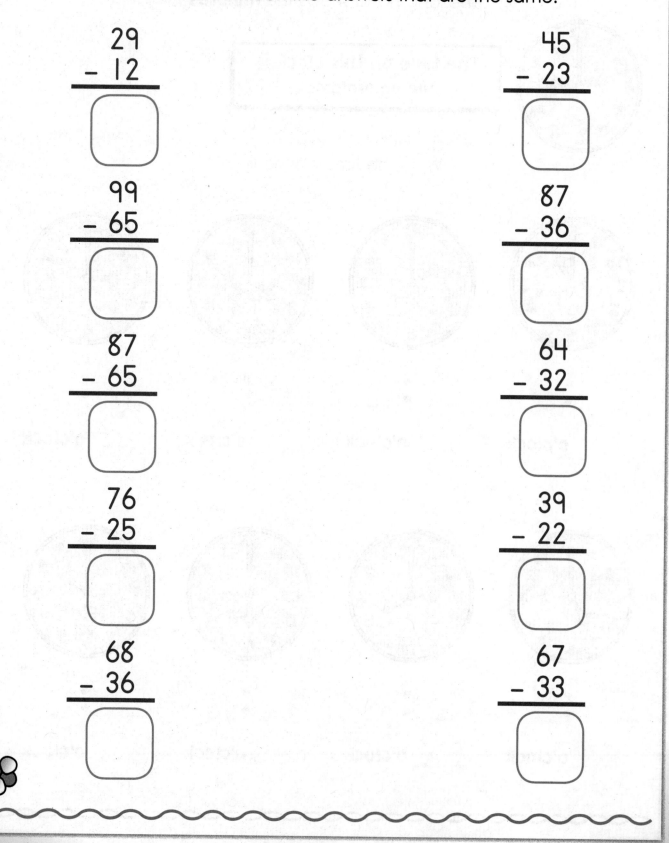

$$
\begin{array}{r} 29 \\ -\ 12 \\ \hline \end{array}
$$

$$
\begin{array}{r} 99 \\ -\ 65 \\ \hline \end{array}
$$

$$
\begin{array}{r} 87 \\ -\ 65 \\ \hline \end{array}
$$

$$
\begin{array}{r} 76 \\ -\ 25 \\ \hline \end{array}
$$

$$
\begin{array}{r} 68 \\ -\ 36 \\ \hline \end{array}
$$

$$
\begin{array}{r} 45 \\ -\ 23 \\ \hline \end{array}
$$

$$
\begin{array}{r} 87 \\ -\ 36 \\ \hline \end{array}
$$

$$
\begin{array}{r} 64 \\ -\ 32 \\ \hline \end{array}
$$

$$
\begin{array}{r} 39 \\ -\ 22 \\ \hline \end{array}
$$

$$
\begin{array}{r} 67 \\ -\ 33 \\ \hline \end{array}
$$

Time on the Half Hour

The short hand of the clock shows the hour.
The long hand shows how many minutes after the hour.
When the minute hand is on the **6**, it is **half past** the hour.

A half hour is 30 minutes.
This clock shows 7:30 or half past 7.

Draw the hands on each clock to show the correct time.

8:00   **7:30**   **6:30**   **12:00**

4:00   **5:30**   **10:30**   **10:00**

9:00   **11:30**   **12:30**   **2:00**

What Makes Sense?

Print a word from the word list that makes sense
in each sentence. Use each word only once.

Word List

hop	bark	duck
roar	bird	fly

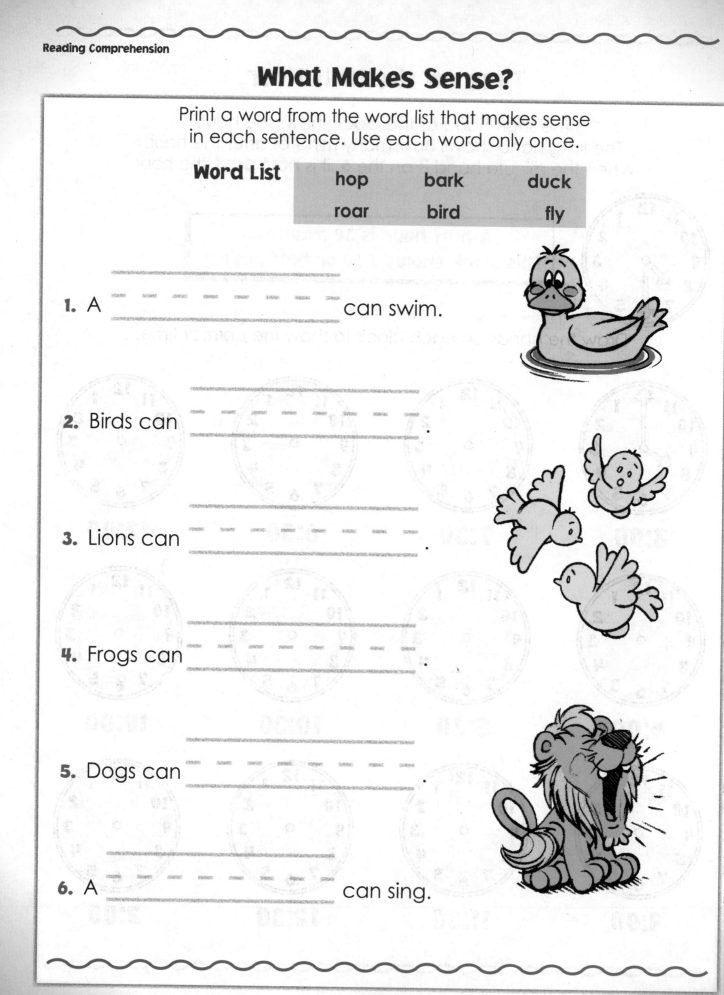

1. A _____ can swim.

2. Birds can _____ .

3. Lions can _____ .

4. Frogs can _____ .

5. Dogs can _____ .

6. A _____ can sing.

Shopping "Cents"

Add the cost of the two items. Write the total in the box.

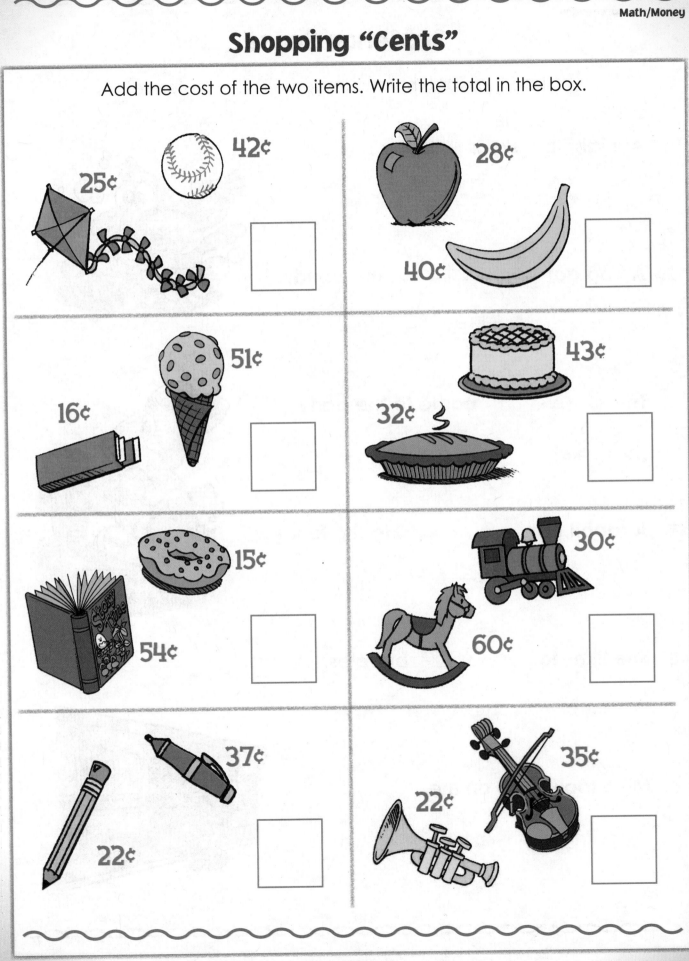

Sentence Sense

Circle the word that makes sense in the sentence.

1. At night, the sky is _____ .

   green   dark   down

2. A frog got _____ in the pond.

   wet   when   hop

3. The _____ came to the party.

   game   sun   girls

4. A rabbit can _____ to the fence.

   hop   hat   boy

5. Sue likes to _____ bubbles.

   food   blow   take

6. Mike took a trip on the _____ .

   swing   school   train

Beginning Digraphs: ch, sh, th

Circle the beginning digraph **ch**, **sh**, or **th**
in each word. Say the word.

1. chew	2. thank	3. three	4. shock	5. shut
6. thumb	7. choose	8. shape	9. chime	10. thing

Look at the picture in each box. Draw a line from
the picture to its name. Circle the beginning digraph.

shirt shine ship	check child chin	thunder thin thread
cheer chick cheap	thimble thumb think	show shoe shop

Read the words in the word list.
Write each word below its beginning digraph.

Word List

chip	shy	thumb
thin	chin	ship

ch	sh	th

Calendar Investigation

Trace the numeral 1. Complete the **calendar** by filling in the missing numerals 2–30. Answer the questions below.

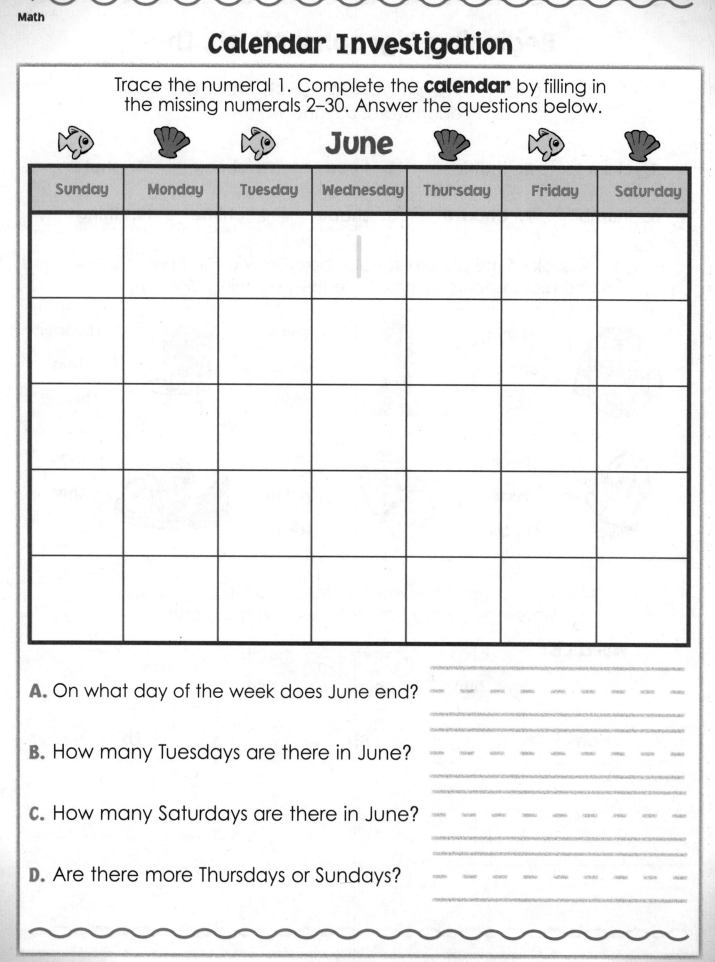

June

Sunday	Monday	Tuesday	Wednesday	Thursday	Friday	Saturday
			1			

A. On what day of the week does June end?

B. How many Tuesdays are there in June?

C. How many Saturdays are there in June?

D. Are there more Thursdays or Sundays?

Syllables

Say the word. Write the number of syllables.

bird _____

apple _____

rabbit _____

wind _____

yellow _____

kitten _____

tree _____

fish _____

marker _____

cat _____

Divide each word into two syllables. The first one is done for you.

little	funny
lit tle	_____ _____
lumber	dinner
_____ _____	_____ _____

Greater/Less

In each box, circle the number that is **greater**.

26 30	41 29	50 20	99 100
11 19	67 57	84 48	72 27
43 34	10 60	50 75	38 28

In each box, circle the number that is **less**.

0 10	70 50	15 30	50 25
48 24	16 32	36 72	40 80
29 58	19 38	42 21	100 50

The Biggest and Best Book about Me!

By

1

Draw a picture of yourself in the frame below. Color the picture.

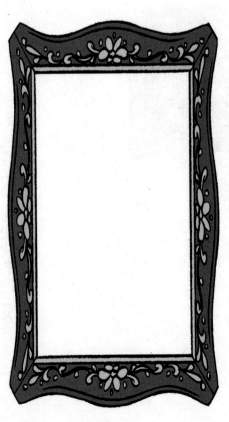

Describe yourself. Use the words in the word list to complete the sentences.

Word List

green	blue	gray
brown	black	red
hazel	long	curly
straight	short	blonde

I have _____ eyes.

I have _____ hair.

My hair is _____ .

3

117

Complete the sentences below. Use the answers to write a story about yourself on a separate sheet of paper.

My name is

My favorite color is.

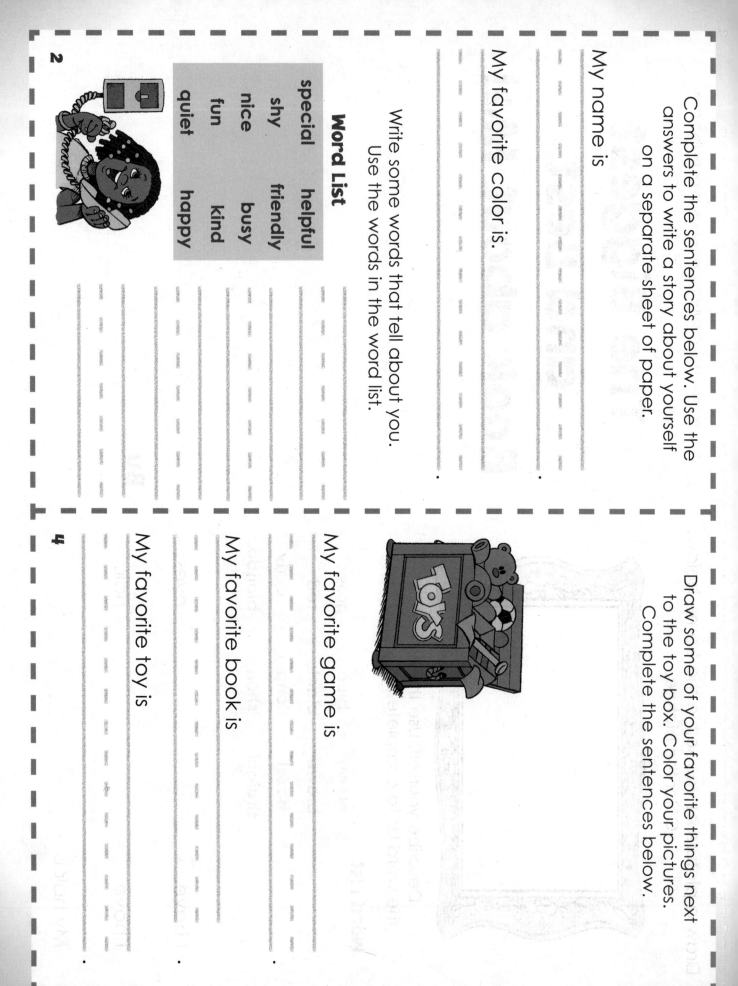

Write some words that tell about you. Use the words in the word list.

Word List

special	helpful
shy	friendly
nice	busy
fun	kind
quiet	happy

2

Draw some of your favorite things next to the toy box. Color your pictures. Complete the sentences below.

My favorite game is

My favorite book is

My favorite toy is

4

Read the sentences. Draw a picture in each box.

This makes me **happy**.	This makes me **angry**.
This **surprises** me.	This makes me **laugh**.
This makes me **scared**.	This makes me **proud**.

5

Tell about your family.

Fill in the correct numbers.

I have . . . ☐ brother(s). ☐ sister(s).

☐ uncle(s). ☐ aunt(s).

☐ cousin(s).

Check one.

I am . . . ☐ the oldest.

☐ in the middle.

☐ the only child.

☐ the youngest.

7

Tell about the pictures you drew on page 5.

I feel **happy** when

_____

I feel **angry** when

_____

I feel **surprised** when

_____

I **laugh** when

_____

I feel **scared** when

_____

I feel **proud** when

_____

6   Today I feel

_____

Families have different rules
to keep everyone safe and happy.
Write some of the rules in your family.

A safety rule in my family is

_____

_____

A cleanup rule in my family is

_____

_____

8

Families have different rules
to keep everyone safe and happy.
Write some of the rules in your family.

A bedtime rule in my family is

_____

_____

_____

A rule just for me is

_____

_____

_____

Complete each sentence.
Draw a picture for each sentence.

My family has fun when

_____

_____

_____

My family works together when

_____

_____

_____

Families work together and help each other. Write about how you help the people in your family.

Every day I _____

_____

_____ .

A special job I have is _____

_____

_____ .

My favorite job is _____

_____

_____ .

I enjoy helping my _____

_____

_____ .

This is a picture of me and my family at home.

Place Value (Hundreds)

Build each number using a place value mat, if you have one.
Write how many hundreds, tens, and ones are in each number.

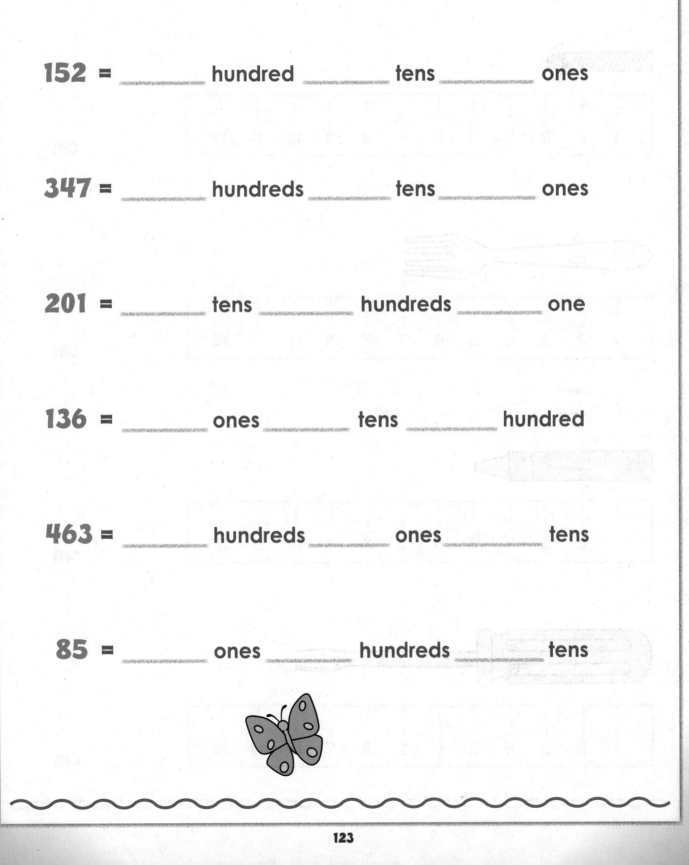

152 = _____ hundred _____ tens _____ ones

347 = _____ hundreds _____ tens _____ ones

201 = _____ tens _____ hundreds _____ one

136 = _____ ones _____ tens _____ hundred

463 = _____ hundreds _____ ones _____ tens

85 = _____ ones _____ hundreds _____ tens

Measuring in Centimeters

Look at each centimeter ruler.
Write the length of each object in **centimeters**.

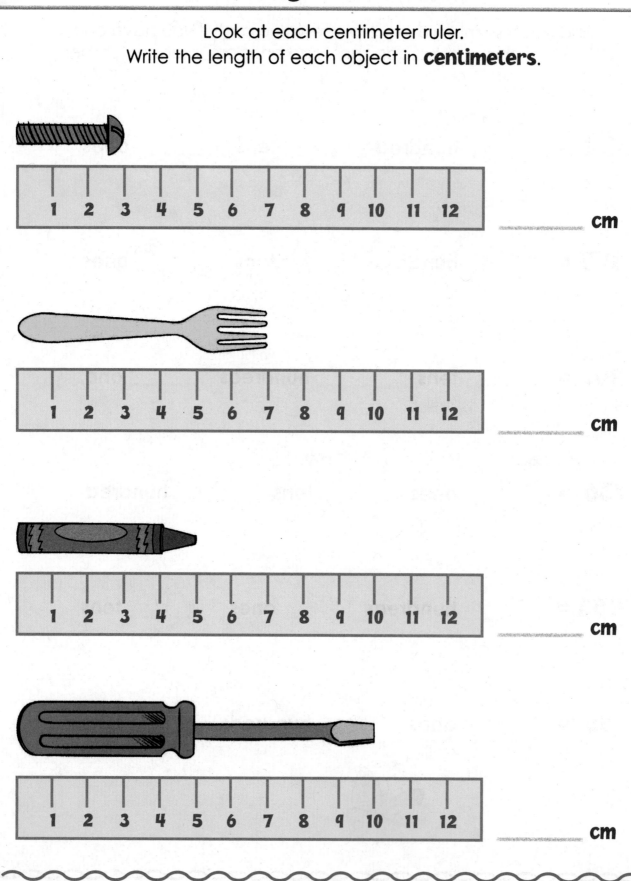

Ending Digraphs: -ch, -sh, -th

Read the words. Circle the ending digraph
ch, **sh**, or **th** in each word.

1. coach	2. dish	3. mouth	4. moth
5. bush	6. couch	7. trash	8. much

Say the name of each picture. Fill in the circle next to the ending digraph.

○ ch
○ sh

○ sh
○ th

○ ch
○ th

Read each sentence. Write the word from the word list
that completes the sentence. Circle the ending digraph.

Word List   month   bush   touch

Your cat is hiding behind the _____ .

Do not _____ the sharp needles of the cactus.

Valentine's Day is in the _____ of February.

Write three words that each end with a different digraph: **ch**, **sh**, or **th**.

_____   _____   _____

_____   _____   _____

Following Directions

Follow the directions to complete the picture.

1. Draw two little ducks behind the others.
2. Color the biggest duck yellow.
3. Draw a plant by the pond.
4. Make a nest near the pond.
5. Color each duck a different color.
6. Circle the smallest duck.
7. Color the water blue.
8. Color the plants green.

Match the Opposites

Draw lines to match the pictures that are **opposites**.

left

day

night

right

dry

sad

happy

wet

Subtraction Review

Fill in the missing numbers.

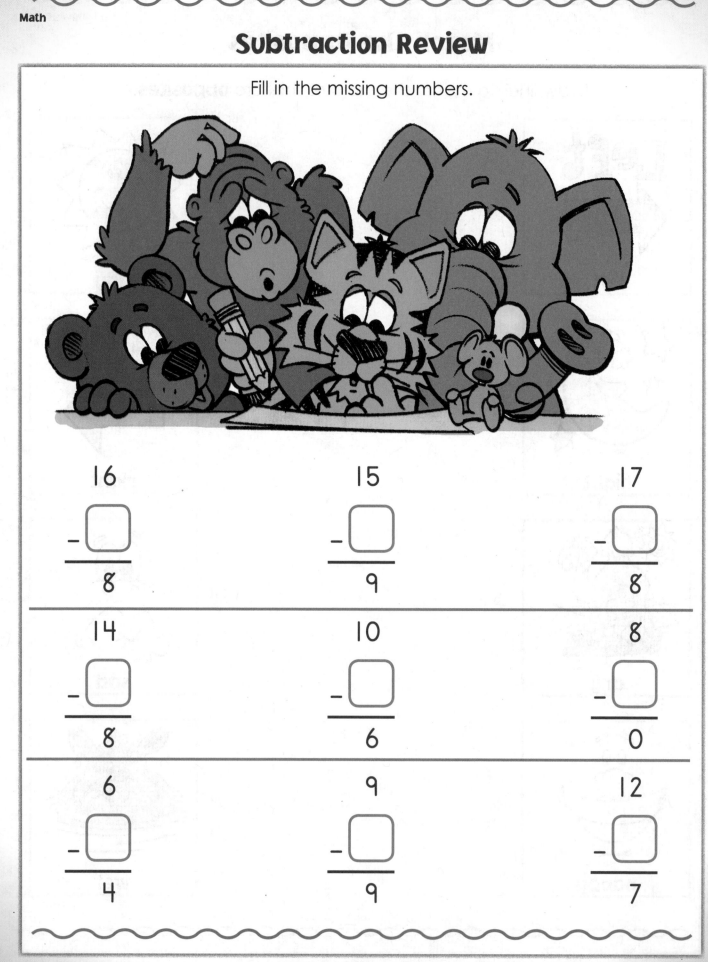

16
− □
8

15
− □
9

17
− □
8

14
− □
8

10
− □
6

8
− □
0

6
− □
4

9
− □
9

12
− □
7

Ending Digraph -ng

Write the **ng** digraph at the end of each set of letters. Say the words.

cla _____

wro _____

bri _____

si _____

lu _____

stro _____

Look at the picture in each box. Write the **ng** word
that names the picture and circle the ending digraph.

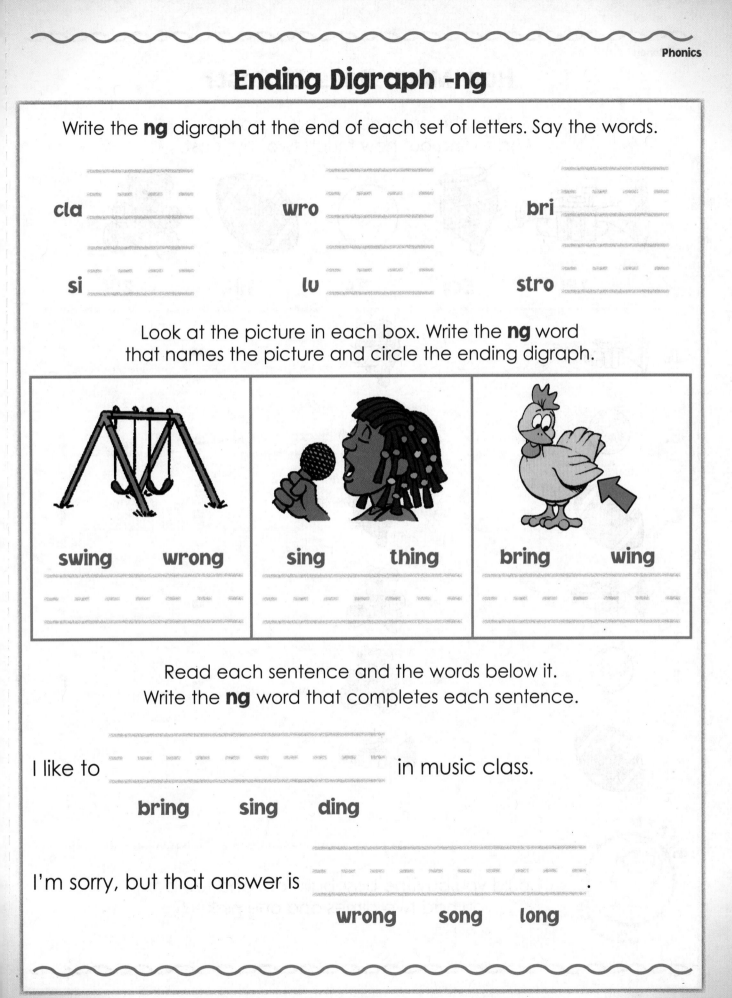

swing   wrong

sing   thing

bring   wing

Read each sentence and the words below it.
Write the **ng** word that completes each sentence.

I like to _____ in music class.

bring   sing   ding

I'm sorry, but that answer is _____ .

wrong   song   long

How Much Does It Cost?

Write the price next to each object.
Add to find out how much two toys cost.

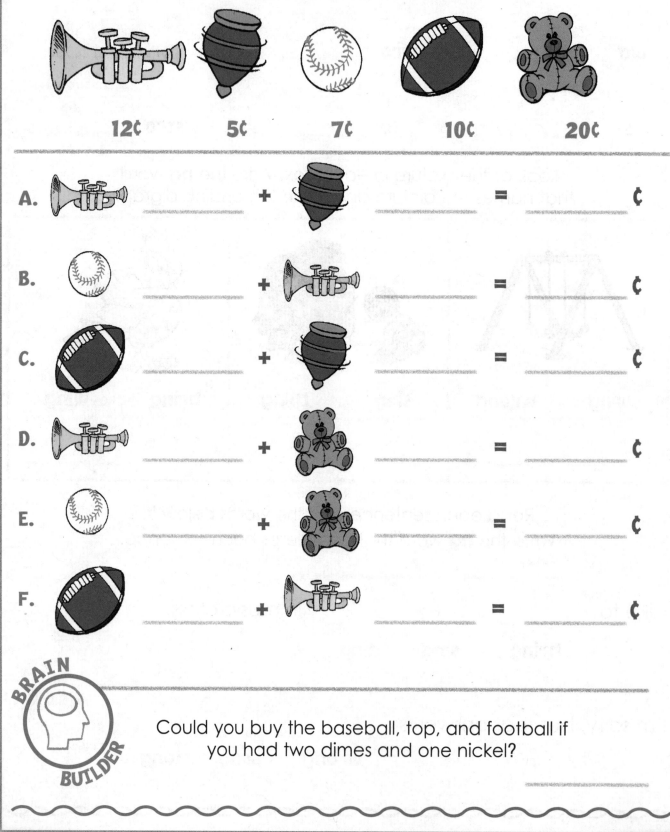

Could you buy the baseball, top, and football if
you had two dimes and one nickel?

Homonym Crossword Puzzle

Homonyms are words that sound alike.
Complete the puzzle using the homonyms from the word list.

Word List

| blue | hear | four | our |
| plane | pail | eight | right |

Across

1. for
4. ate
6. plain
7. blew

Down

2. hour
3. write
5. here
6. pale

131

Three-Addend Addition

Sometimes in addition, **three** numbers are added together.
To find the sum, add the first two addends together,
then add the third addend.

4 + 3 + 5 = 12
Think . . . 4 + 3 = ⬚7⬚ , then ⬚7⬚ + 5 = 12

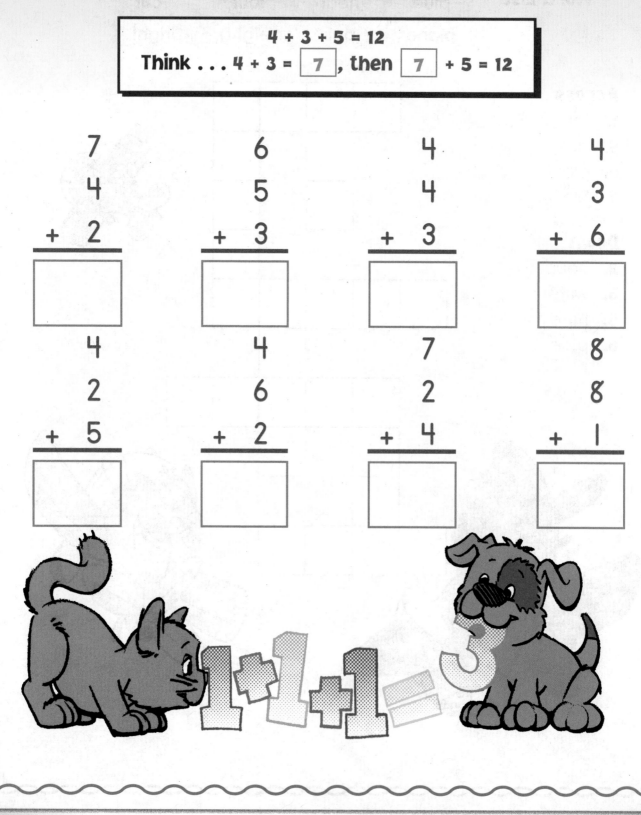

```
   7          6          4          4
   4          5          4          3
 + 2        + 3        + 3        + 6
 ┌────┐     ┌────┐     ┌────┐     ┌────┐
 │    │     │    │     │    │     │    │
 └────┘     └────┘     └────┘     └────┘

   4          4          7          8
   2          6          2          8
 + 5        + 2        + 4        + 1
 ┌────┐     ┌────┐     ┌────┐     ┌────┐
 │    │     │    │     │    │     │    │
 └────┘     └────┘     └────┘     └────┘
```

Ending Digraph Review: -ch, -sh, -th, -ng

Say each word. Fill in the circle if the word
ends with the digraph **ch**, **sh**, **th**, or **ng**.

◯ junk   ◯ king   ◯ sandwich   ◯ hat

◯ booth   ◯ glee   ◯ most   ◯ wish

Say the name of each picture. Circle the correct ending digraph.

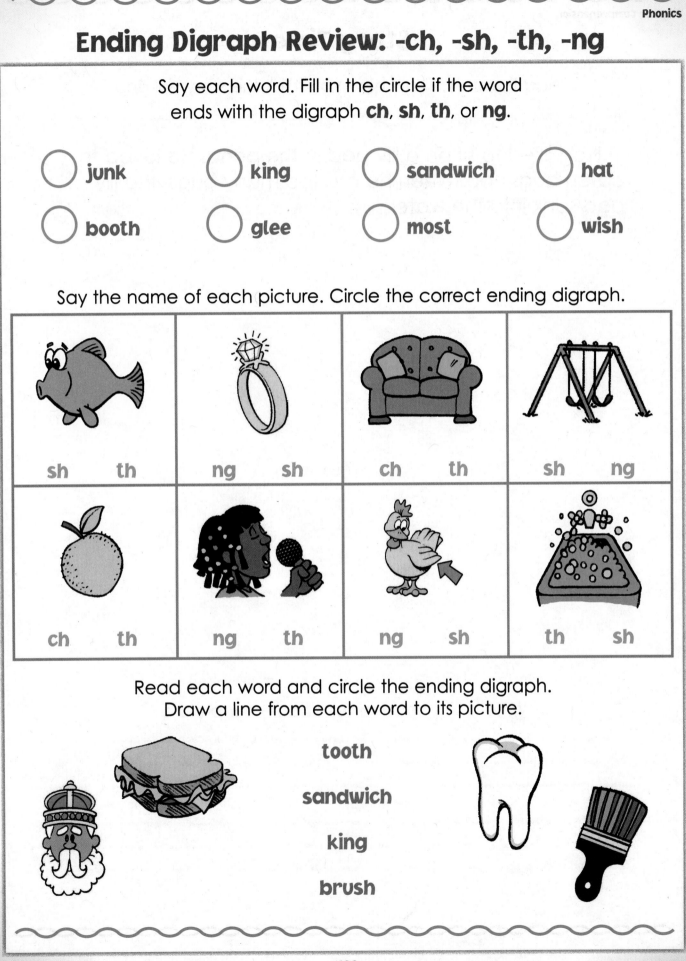

sh th	ng sh	ch th	sh ng
ch th	ng th	ng sh	th sh

Read each word and circle the ending digraph.
Draw a line from each word to its picture.

tooth

sandwich

king

brush

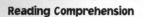

Story Time

Read the story. Draw how you think the story will end.

Frog liked to sit on a lily pad in the pond. He loved to catch bugs, too. When he ate too many bugs, the lily pad sank into the water.

Write a sentence to tell about your picture.

Fractions (½)

Color ½ of each shape.

Brian had six mini pizzas for his party. He cut each pizza in half. How many halves did he have in all?

R-Controlled Vowel ar

Say the name of each picture. Listen to the **ar** sound.

car   card

Look at the words in the word list.
Write each word on the line next to the correct picture.

Word List   shark   barn   bark   star   jar   yarn

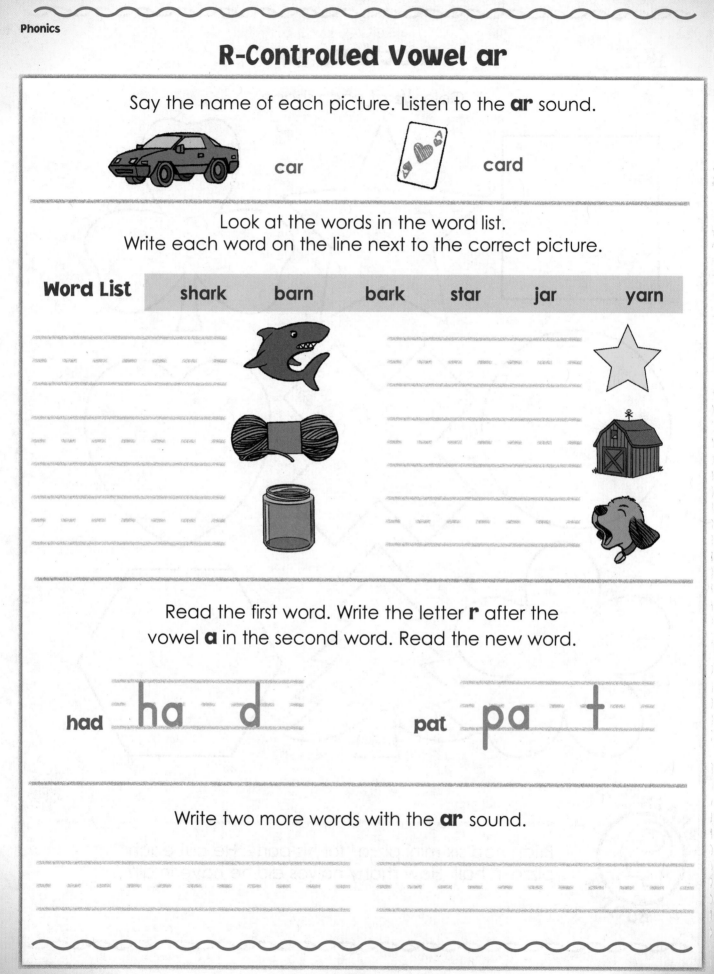

Read the first word. Write the letter **r** after the
vowel **a** in the second word. Read the new word.

had   ha   d   pat   pa   t

Write two more words with the **ar** sound.

Hit the Target Math

Subtract. Cut out and glue the arrow
with the correct answer to each target.

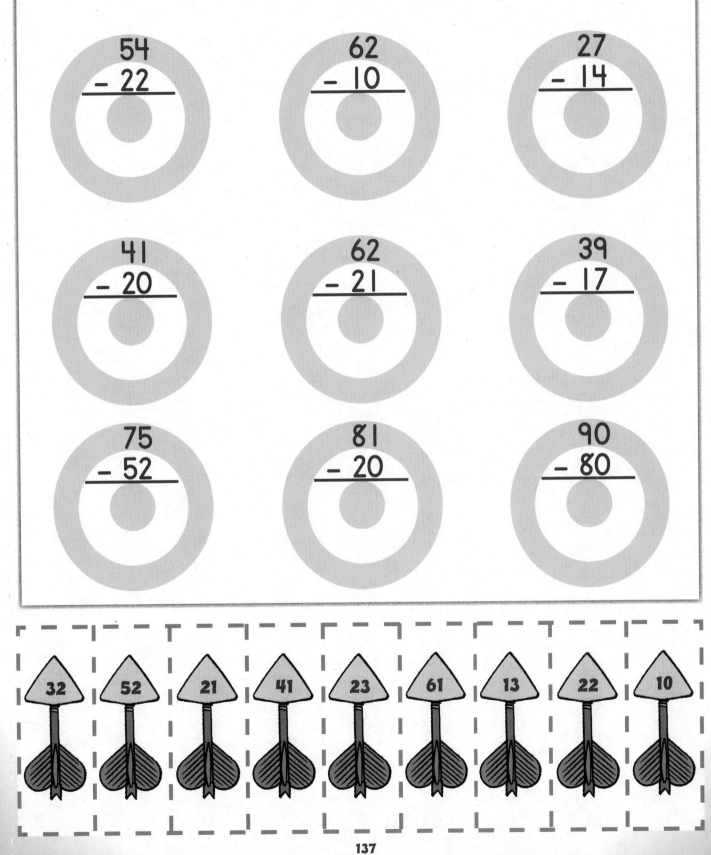

Remove pages 139–142. Cut along dashed lines. Staple pages in order. See directions on page 142.

My Own Story

Written and Illustrated by

_____

1

3

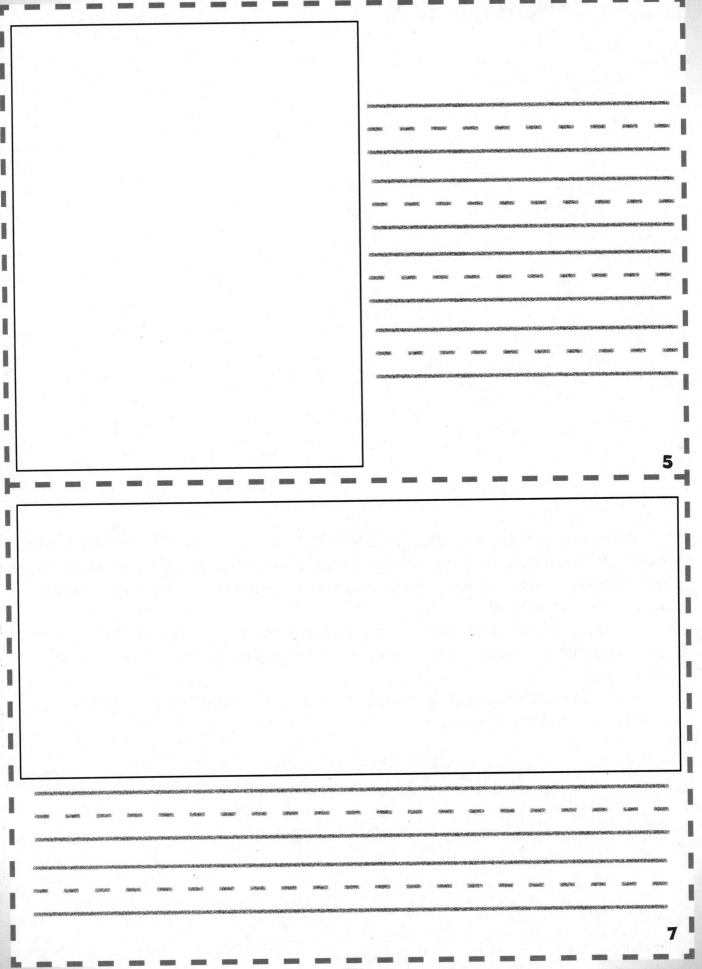

5

7

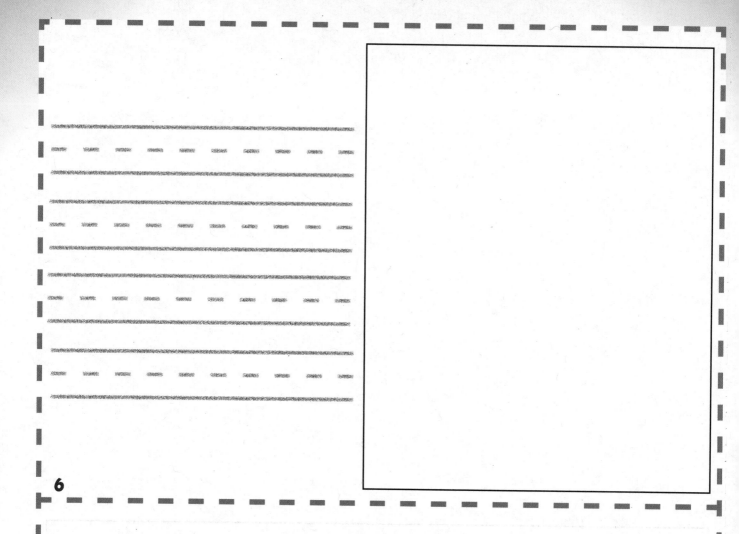

6

You have permission to photocopy pages 139–142. Let your child practice writing and illustrating a story. For many children entering second grade, six pages will be too many pages to write. Let your child decide how long and how many pages the story will be when it is finished.

Do not "over-correct." To become a good writer, one has to practice. Children who are overly criticized will not want to practice, and writing could become an unpleasant experience.

Encourage your child to be creative and imaginative. Help your child discover how much fun it is to learn to write!

Coloring Fractions

Color the objects divided into **halves** red.
Color the objects divided into **thirds** blue.
Color the objects divided into **fourths** green.

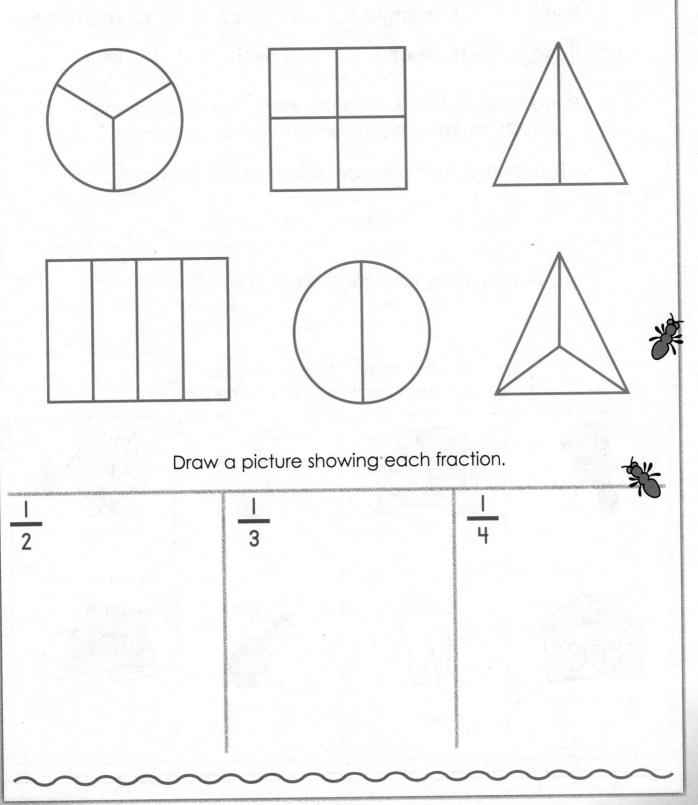

Draw a picture showing each fraction.

$\dfrac{1}{2}$ | $\dfrac{1}{3}$ | $\dfrac{1}{4}$

Beginning and Ending Digraphs

Read the words. Circle the beginning or ending digraph in each word.

1. cheese	2. south	3. ring	4. crush
5. think	6. shingle	7. touch	8. shampoo
9. thorn	10. such	11. wish	12. sing

Read each sentence. Write the words that begin or end
with **ch**, **sh**, **th**, or **ng** digraphs. Circle each digraph.

The mouse had a piece of cheese in its mouth.

A very short king must wear a small robe.

Say the name of each picture.
Write the correct beginning or ending digraph.

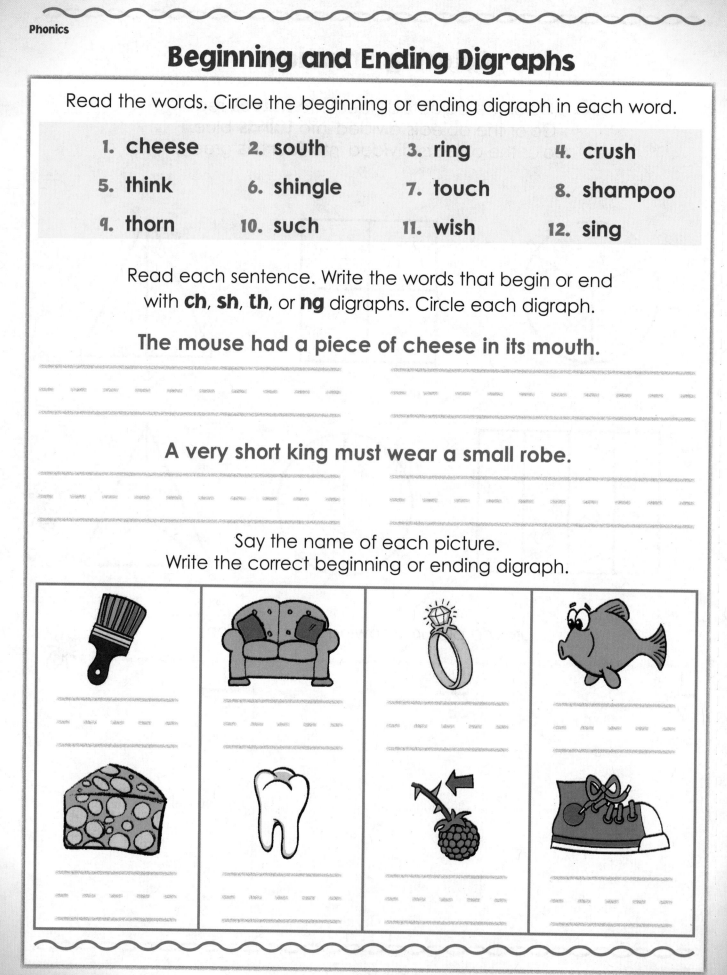

Fraction Practice

Circle the fraction shown in each picture.

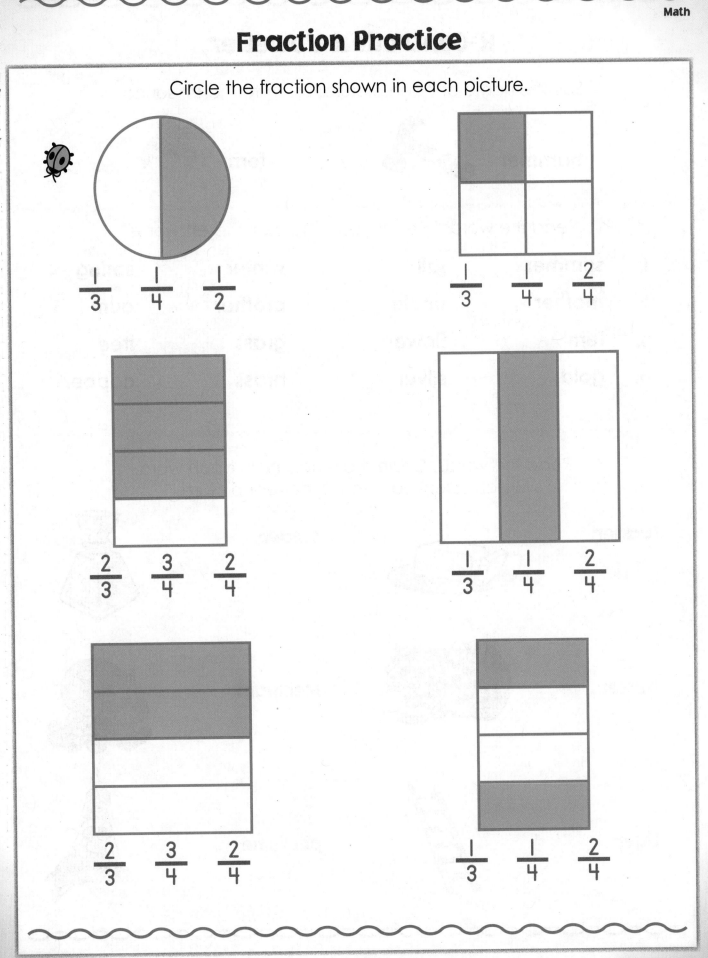

$\dfrac{1}{3}$ $\dfrac{1}{4}$ $\dfrac{1}{2}$

$\dfrac{1}{3}$ $\dfrac{1}{4}$ $\dfrac{2}{4}$

$\dfrac{2}{3}$ $\dfrac{3}{4}$ $\dfrac{2}{4}$

$\dfrac{1}{3}$ $\dfrac{1}{4}$ $\dfrac{2}{4}$

$\dfrac{2}{3}$ $\dfrac{3}{4}$ $\dfrac{2}{4}$

$\dfrac{1}{3}$ $\dfrac{1}{4}$ $\dfrac{2}{4}$

R-Controlled Vowel er

Say the name of each picture. Listen to the **er** sound.

hammer

fern

Read the words in each row. Circle all the **er** words.

1.	summer	fall	winter	spring
2.	mother	uncle	brother	aunt
3.	fern	flower	grass	tree
4.	gold	silver	brass	copper

Read the words. Circle the letters **er** in each word.
Match each word to the correct picture.

ladder

butter

tiger

spider

mermaid

perfume

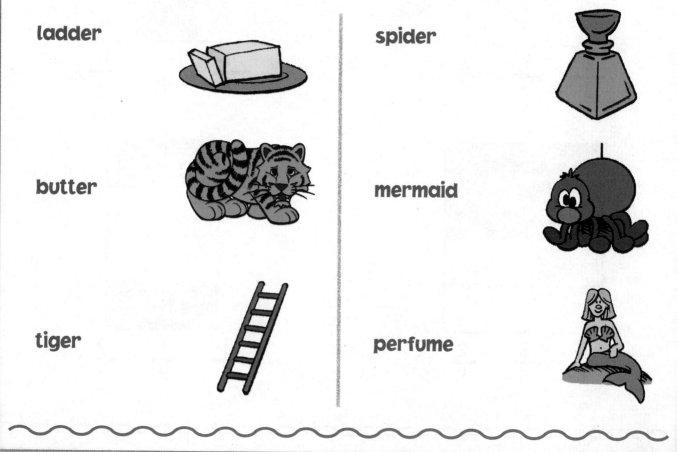

R-Controlled Vowel ir

Say the name of each picture. Listen to the **ir** sound.

girl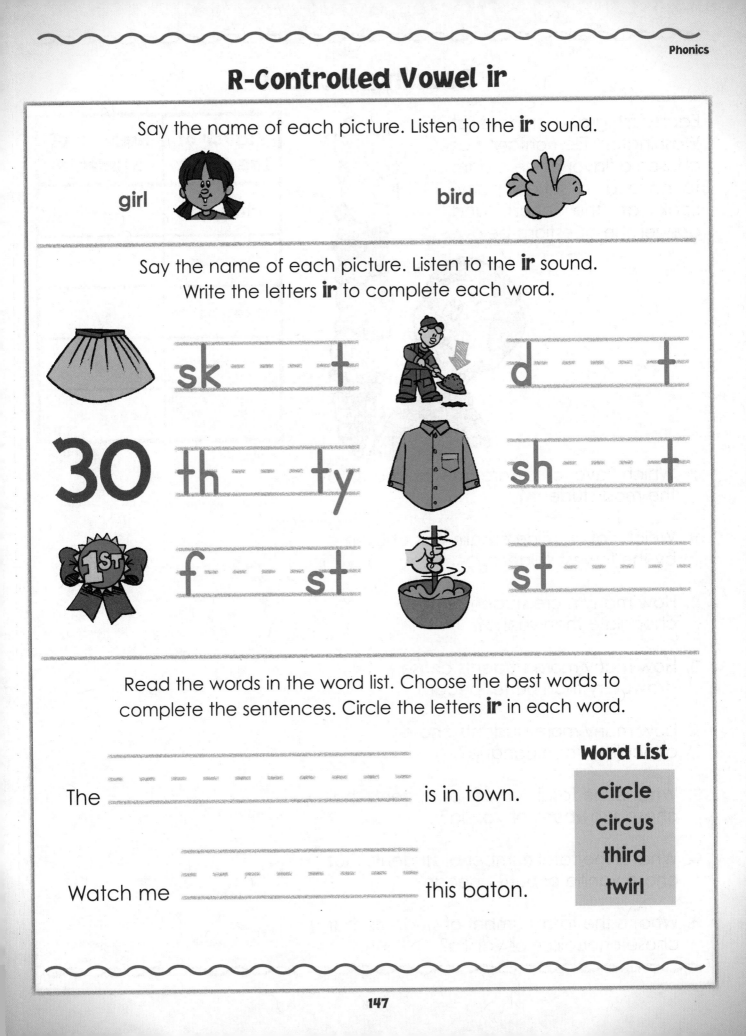

bird

Say the name of each picture. Listen to the **ir** sound.
Write the letters **ir** to complete each word.

sk _ _ t

d _ _ t

th _ _ ty

sh _ _ t

f _ _ st

st _ _ _

Read the words in the word list. Choose the best words to
complete the sentences. Circle the letters **ir** in each word.

The _____ is in town.

Watch me _____ this baton.

Word List

circle

circus

third

twirl

Reading a Chart

Each first grade student at Washington Elementary has chosen a flavor of ice cream to have at a school party. Look at the chart and answer the questions below.

Flavor of Ice Cream	Number of Students
chocolate	47
vanilla	32
strawberry	17
banana	10
butter pecan	5

A. Which flavor of ice cream was chosen by the most students?

B. Which flavor of ice cream was chosen by the fewest students?

C. How many more students chose chocolate than vanilla?

D. How many more students chose strawberry than butter pecan?

E. How many more students chose chocolate than banana?

F. What is the total number of students that chose strawberry or vanilla?

G. What is the total number of students that chose vanilla or butter pecan?

H. What is the total number of students that chose chocolate or vanilla?

R-Controlled Vowel or

Say the name of each picture. Listen to the **or** sound.

horn  fork

Read the words. Circle the letters **or** in each word.
Match each word to the correct picture.

porch

storm

stork

cork

acorn

cord

store

snore

Say the name of each picture.
Circle the picture in each pair whose name has the **or** sound.

R-Controlled Vowel ur

Say the name of each picture. Listen to the **ur** sound.

turkey 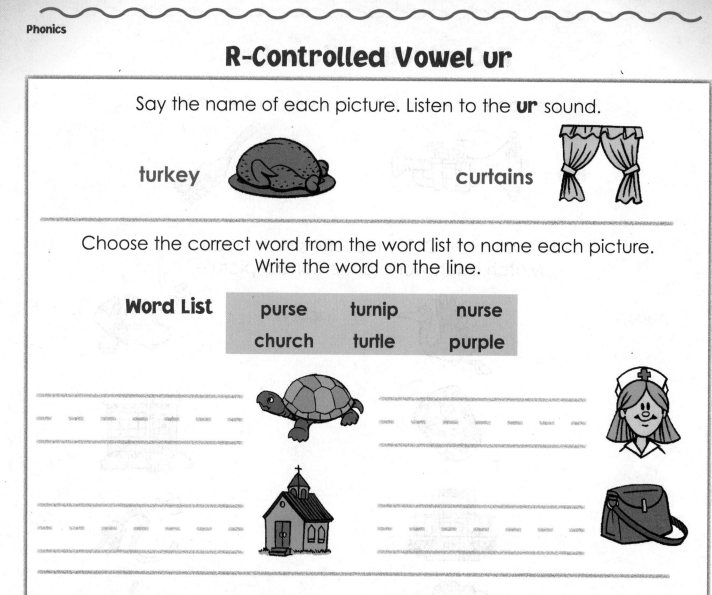 curtains

Choose the correct word from the word list to name each picture.
Write the word on the line.

Word List

purse	turnip	nurse
church	turtle	purple

Read each sentence. Circle the **ur** word in each sentence.

1. We had turkey for dinner.

2. The school nurse treated me.

3. Please return the books to Tim.

4. I hurt my leg when I fell.

5. Will you please turn on the radio?

Cut-and-Paste Synonyms

Synonyms are words that have the same or nearly the same meaning. Cut and paste to match the synonyms.

happy

ill

couch

angry

skinny

friends

sick

mad

thin

pals

glad

sofa

Money Problems

Solve the word problems.

A. Susan had a nickel. She found another nickel. Her mother gave her two dimes for taking out the trash. How much money does she have now?

_____ ¢

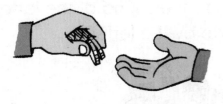

B. Tyrone wants to buy ice cream at lunch. Lunch costs 50¢ and ice cream costs 25¢. If Tyrone has $1.00, does he have enough to buy both?

Yes   **No**

C. Maria took 50¢ to the store. She spent 10¢ on candy, 10¢ on popcorn, and 15¢ on a drink. How much money did she spend?

_____ ¢

How much does she have left?

_____ ¢

Y as a Vowel

When **y** is at the end of a word,
it can make the long sound of the vowel **e** or **i**.

baby (ē)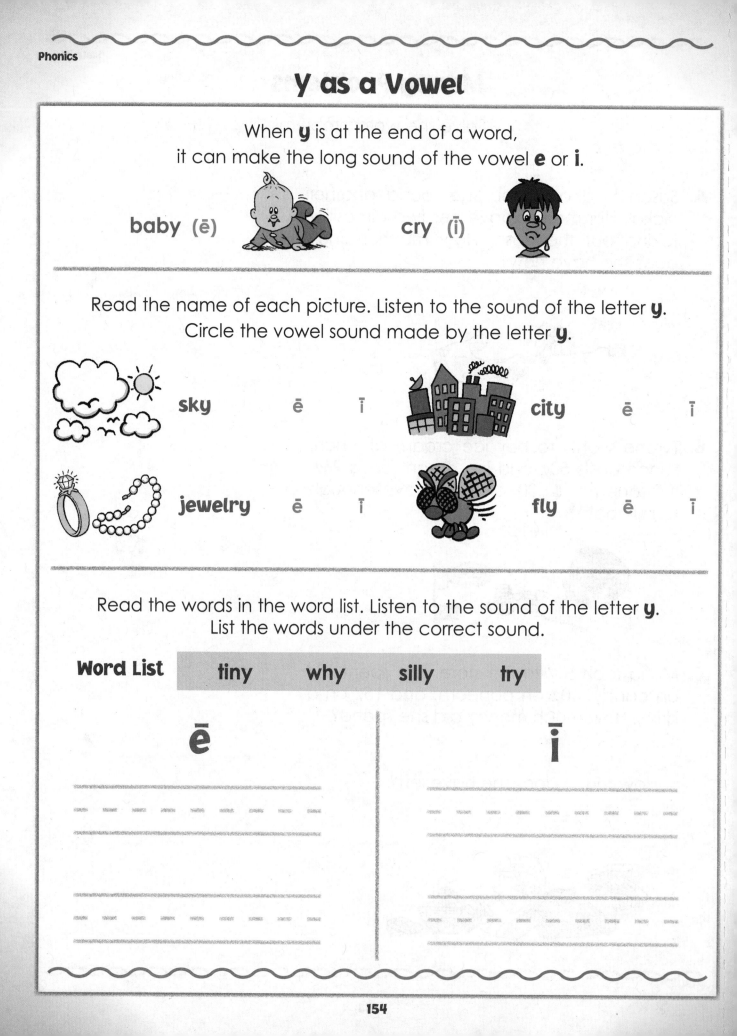

cry (ī)

Read the name of each picture. Listen to the sound of the letter **y**.
Circle the vowel sound made by the letter **y**.

sky   ē   ī

city   ē   ī

jewelry   ē   ī

fly   ē   ī

Read the words in the word list. Listen to the sound of the letter **y**.
List the words under the correct sound.

Word List   tiny   why   silly   try

ē	ī

Cut-and-Paste Antonyms

Antonyms are words that have opposite meanings.
Cut and paste to match the antonyms.

in

little

hard

cold

back

empty

front

out

full

big

hot

soft

Reproducible Creative Writing Paper

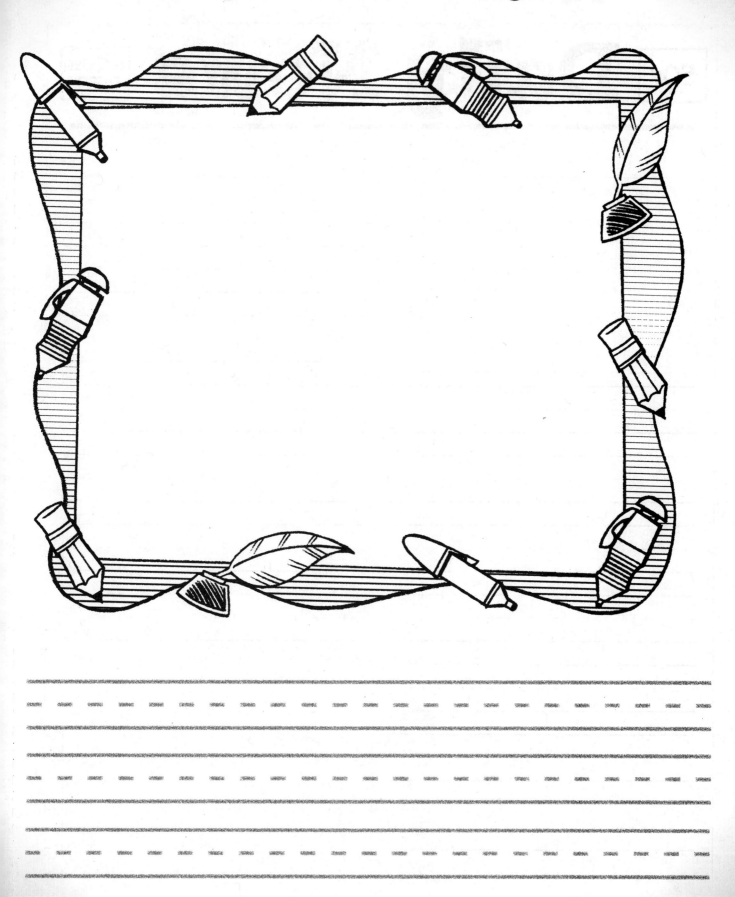

50¢ Daily News

MORNING EDITION

Cut-and-Color Awards

Parent: Have your child decorate and color these awards. Fill in your child's name and the date to mark each accomplishment. The awards can be worn as badges or put into small frames.

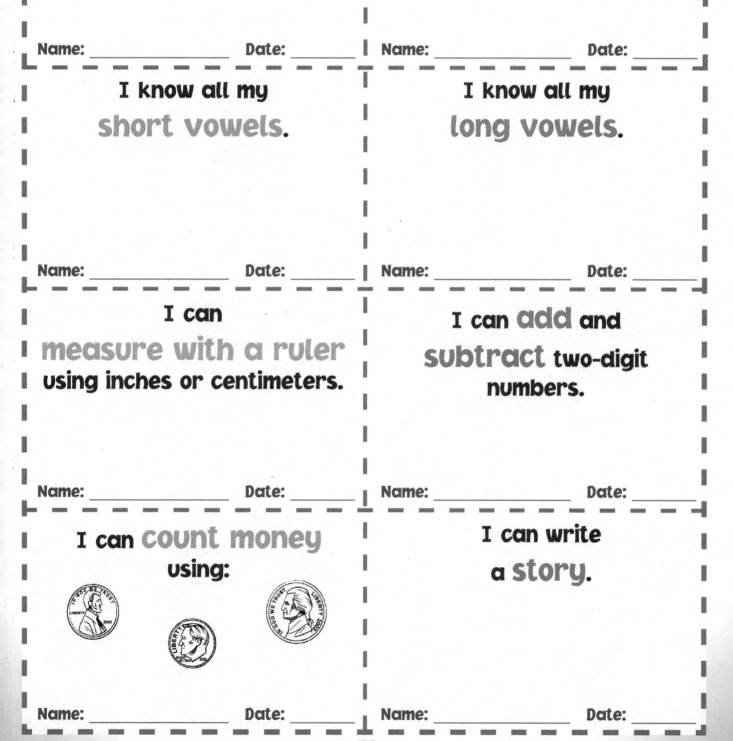

I can **tell time** on the hour and half hour.

Name: _____ Date: _____

I know my **+** and **−** facts to 20.

Name: _____ Date: _____

I know all my **short vowels**.

Name: _____ Date: _____

I know all my **long vowels**.

Name: _____ Date: _____

I can **measure with a ruler** using inches or centimeters.

Name: _____ Date: _____

I can **add** and **subtract** two-digit numbers.

Name: _____ Date: _____

I can **count money** using:

Name: _____ Date: _____

I can write **a story**.

Name: _____ Date: _____